"As one of America's most qualified proponents of cell ministry, my friend Billy Hornsby ushers us in to new dimensions of blessing and church growth through this exciting new book. If you are looking for a reliable source of practical information on the Spirit's current emphasis of mobilizing God's people for ministry, you have found it. Keep it close by, for you will refer to it over and over as you build for God."

Dr. David Cannistraci
Senior Pastor
Evangel Christian Fellowship, San Jose, California

"Billy Hornsby has done a masterful job in communicating cell-church principles necessary for building an effective and successful Church in the twenty-first century. His years of experience, Biblical knowledge, and wisdom portray some of the most thought-provoking concepts that demand the attention of every pastor and leader in the church today. This book will help every church, regardless of its size, to fulfill its mandate as a New Testament church and reap the fruit of harvest."

Marc Estes
Director of Pastoral and Harvest Ministries
City Bible Church, Portland, Oregon

"Billy Hornsby really has a handle on the "How To's" of cells and leadership development in the local church. The principles in this book are helping us to hold the harvest that God is giving and to train new leaders for tomorrow. Great stuff!"

Pastor Greg Surratt
Seacoast Church - Mt. Pleasant, SC

"Here's a blueprint for multiplying your congregation. Proven in the trenches, refined by what works, this book blows past the theories of church growth, taking its readers into an attainable harvest. See how once-disaffected believers are consumed by God's call to make disciples. It's so natural and doable you'll kick yourself for not having done it sooner."

Francis Anfuso
Senior Pastor- The Rock of Roseville
Roseville, CA

The Cell·Driven Church

Realizing the Harvest

by **Billy Hornsby**

Fire Wind™

Mansfield, PA

Published by Kingdom Publishing
© 2000 by Billy Hornsby
ISBN: 1-883906-47-4
Printed in the U. S. A.
ALL RIGHTS RESERVED

Kingdom Publishing
719 Lambs Creek Road
Mansfield, PA 16933

(800) 597-1123

Table of Contents

Dedication

After eight years of working in the cell-group ministry I have learned to appreciate the many people that it takes on all levels to make it successful. I dedicate this book to the following.

The Lord Jesus, for His love for me and revelation that He gives for such an important work.

To my wife, Charlene, who always "felt" that this book should be written and would be published. She personally sacrificed time with me for the sake of the cell-group ministry and this book. She is the great cheerleader in my life.

To my "behind the scenes" helper Gayle Bennett, my secretary, who, with such a great attitude, labored endless hours to make it "happen." To Nancy Lambert, the editor at Kingdom Publishing, for her enthusiasm about the importance of the book and her work to make it readable.

Next, to all of the District and Zone Pastors at Bethany World Prayer Center who so diligently worked above and beyond the call of duty to train leaders and open new cell groups. Without their work the cell-church concept would not have become a reality.

Then to the cell leaders at Bethany who proved over and over again that they possessed the "gift of God" that was necessary to reach souls and build a successful cell church. They became the examples to our nation of what the "lay person" could accomplish for God.

Also, to Dr. Ralph Neighbour, who kept the vision for the cell church alive in the 20th century and for his dedication to the worldwide cell-church movement.

Finally, to Pastor Larry Stockstill who kept the vision for the transition into the cell-church model and for his personal commitment to exposing the nation to the possibilities for growth of local churches through the cell-church model.

Foreword

Having been with Billy Hornsby in Kazakstan and then in part of Usbekistan and seeing and hearing his passion to reach and disciple souls is awesome. I have never seen anyone more passionate to develop group leaders.

This book is not only life changing, it is nation changing.

Certainly the principles that he teaches we have already applied in our local church and I see them working all over the world.

If we are to reach our generation, we must have a plan. Here is the plan.

Marilyn Hickey

A Word From...

Pastor Larry Stockstill

Brother Hornsby's book, *The Cell-Driven Church*, answers the "Why" and "How To" of cell ministry. In his down-home style, he has written an easy-to-digest handbook on the cell structure, with an insider's view as to how God has worked in Bethany World Prayer Center.

Brother Hornsby's book not only casts the cell vision, but is also a great nuts-and-bolts handbook for pastors and Christian workers alike. If you are investigating the cell structure, transitioning to cells or planting a cell church, this is the book for you.

Introduction

This book was originally envisioned as a manual but has migrated somewhat in the writing process. While still a cell-church blueprint, personal vision and testimonies are included to help present the real-life picture of a twenty-first-century New Testament church.

Many details of how a cell church functions and some of the insights that I have personally gleaned over the years are presented to help the reader better understand his/her role as a leader or member of a cell group. We must never forget, however, that it is the work of God; and we are totally dependent on His presence and His creative power to make what we do successful. Take the element of God's intervention out of the formula and all that you have left is another attempt of man to do the work of the Divine. The end result is another program that wears heavy on the local church body to accomplish the impossible without Him.

With Him, the cell-church structure as outlined here helps bring people in contact with each other and the Christ that indwells every believer. It provides us with a highway to travel on and a road map to every destination on that highway. It is my prayer that you arrive at every place that God has intended for you to experience life and ministry at its fullest potential and blessing.

Billy Hornsby
Baker, Louisiana

Note—This book can be read independently or as a companion volume to Pastor Larry Stockstill's book *The Cell Church*.

Chapter 1

Lessons from El Salvador

A Changed Life

The year was 1993, and even after eighteen years of ministry, I had never been involved in "small group" ministry and never intended to be. Oh, I taught an occasional Bible study group in my home, but that was different. I had heard the horror stories about leaders who lead the sheep away from the church one fold at a time, groups that assassinate the pastor, and ingrown cliques that develop in many small-group settings.

Frankly, such accounts made me very suspicious that cell groups could be a tool of the enemy. But that was before I visited an evangelistic cell church in El Salvador.

As you can imagine, I was not "real anxious" to make this visit, but God and Pastor Larry Stockstill had other plans. I had joined the staff of Bethany World Prayer Center in Baker, Louisiana two years earlier, and I was deeply committed to their vision to reach the lost in our town and nearby Baton Rouge. Our church's earlier history was one of tremendous conversion growth, but in recent years that growth had slowed substantially. We earnestly sought God, asking Him what we needed to do to win our city.

His answer was to send us a whole new battle plan.[1] Some eye-opening strategies were revealed to us during a visit from two missionaries to Mexico, Ruth Ann Ost Martinez and her husband Victor Martinez. They had spent some time with the pastor at Misión Elim in the capital city of San Salvador and had observed firsthand his remarkable cell church in action. The story they shared with Pastor Larry, Bethany's senior pastor moved all of us and served as yet another confirmation to the visions and teaching on this topic that our senior pastor had received.

He decided that Bethany was to start the transition to a cell church, and to facilitate this process, Staff Pastor Ron Kairdolf and I were

---

[1] For the full and fascinating account of this plan, I refer you to Larry Stockstill's book, *The Cell Church: Preparing Your Church for the Coming Harvest,* published by Regal.

assigned to visit the work in El Salvador. Initially I went there with a reluctant spirit regarding cells, not realizing that what I experienced there would totally change my life and my philosophy of New Testament ministry.

Six Principles Learned in El Salvador

* **Servanthood** — My first impression of the ministry in San Salvador was not formed by the size of the crowds or the efficiency of the organization. Although these would eventually convince me of the effectiveness of cell-group ministry, it was the *spirit of servanthood* that first caught my attention.

At the time of our visit, the annual meeting of all the cell groups of Elim was in full swing, and over 80,000 people had crammed into a major soccer stadium for this great event. Pastors from all over Central, South, and North America were there. We had arrived right in the middle of the biggest event of the year for this church and expected that for the next few days, we would simply be bystanders amidst tens of thousands of people. I worried that no one would be available to answer our questions.

Upon landing in San Salvador, Ron and I checked into a hotel that seemed to be nice enough for the three or four days that we would be there. We didn't expect a "red carpet" welcome. No one really knew we were coming, except a couple of secretaries and some support staff of the church at Elim. Our instructions were that someone from Misión Elim would pick us up, show us around, and then take us back to our rooms each day.

When the brothers from the church came to pick us up that next morning, however, we were informed that the pastor had a better place for us to stay and that we should check out. They then brought us to the Presidente, a beautiful five-star hotel. They waited patiently while we registered and checked in, and then the brothers escorted us to the church to witness a service.

Before the meeting started, we were given a tour of the church, and many of the aspects of cell-group ministry were explained. Impressed and blessed by the way they served us, I sensed a stirring in me that this was the way the New Testament Church was designed to function.

- **Humility** — A minimum of 10,000 adults was at this particular meeting, and the senior pastor preached an inspiring message to the church. After the church service, I asked if I could possibly meet with the senior pastor. The coordinator of the cell ministry told me, "Of course, wait here." Within a couple of minutes the senior pastor came out of his office, greeted me, and asked if I wanted to talk with him. We then went to a private room where we sat and talked for approximately thirty minutes. He invited Ron and me to go out for dinner with some of his staff, took us to a nice restaurant, and treated us to a wonderful meal. The next day, that very pastor came to the hotel, picked us up, and took Ron and me to a beachfront home of one of the businessmen in his church. There, he spent the entire day graciously answering our questions and encouraging us with the vision of cell-group ministry. Even though he was responsible for the care of nearly 100,000 believers, he still made the effort to be with us and to humbly and personally care for us.

- **Giving** — After the meeting at the beachfront home, we were again taken out to eat, and the staff who went with us continued to answer our questions. When we left to return to the United States a couple of days later, we found out that all our expenses at the hotel had been paid for by Misión Elim of San Salvador! I felt as if I were the most important person in San Salvador that weekend! The Christians at that church served us in a way that I had never been served before. Not only did they shower us with time and attention, but they even paid our expenses. If cell-group ministry could produce radical servants like that, then we might have found the blueprint for our battle plan. This could definitely be the reason for the evangelical success they had. I was excited about the possibilities for our own church and our city.

- **Accountability** — There was another factor that stood out at Misión Elim: a degree of accountability at every level of leadership and by every participant in the "family" groups. I learned weekly reports were generated that not only recorded the numerical element but also reflected the human element. There was a definite sense that the quality of the groups was more important than the quantity of attendees. Every member of the church was accountable to evangelize, to grow spiritually, and to fulfill his own part of the vision to the fullest measure of his capacity. This not only included evangelism and church attendance but also encompassed ministry to each other and to the area around each family group.

Although there were close controls in the organizational structure, the controls were obviously there for the good and the health of the cell groups. This resulted in each person feeling that he was an instrument in God's hand being used to touch the nation of El Salvador for Christ.

- **Purpose** — The most amazing aspect of the cell-group ministry that we observed at Misión Elim was the effective manner in which the vision permeated the entire church structure. Every individual was possessed by the vision of the church. The vision was communicated in a statement of purpose that our pastors at Bethany have since memorized and are now trying to implement in our own cell-group structure. This statement is as follows:

> - Every Christian has a **purpose.**
> - The **purpose** of every Christian is to win the lost to Christ.
> - That **purpose** is best fulfilled in groups where there is accountability and encouragement.
> - The Christian will never be satisfied if he does not fulfill his **purpose** in life.
> - We have no promise of tomorrow. If the **purpose** of the Christian is not being fulfilled now, it may never be.

As we questioned each person with whom we came in contact, we were amazed that each one not only knew the vision of the church but could also quote it back to us. In each cell-group meeting, this vision was rehearsed over and again so that it was never lost. The pastor told us that the way to keep the groups on course and motivated was by having "super vision"! This means that the church must not only provide oversight but must also take responsibility for constantly casting before the congregation the vision of taking the city and the country for Christ.

- **A New Paradigm** — By the time I left El Salvador, I was hooked. The cell church that I witnessed was my first experience in what I now believe to be the New Testament pattern for ministry. It changed me and it opened my eyes as to how the church must reach the world for Christ. You see, this paradigm, or model, of local church expression carries with it not only the powerful evangelistic thrust of the Early Church but also **the very personality of Jesus Christ**. Servanthood, humility,

giving, and accountability all point to His example and His lordship satu-
rating every aspect of our lives.

In the following chapters, I will unroll the battle plan we have implemented at Bethany. You'll find that we have learned much since first catching the vision at Misión Elim in El Salvador.

Chapter 2

What's the Big Idea?

What's the big idea? Small groups in the Church of Jesus Christ have been around since the day of Pentecost. For years, experts on church growth have taught on small groups in conferences and seminars, and scores of books have been written on the subject. So why is there now so much excitement all over the world about cell groups? I saw tremendous results in San Salvador, but could this cell-church model also work in Baker, Louisiana?

Even though small groups have been around for years, they have been only a part of the total focus of local church ministry. Consequently, the idea of cell groups as a main focus for all aspects of local church ministry is a concept that has had little place in the local church in America until now. Although his is a model that many churches have tried to emulate, Dr. David Yonggi Cho's model of a cell group church in Seoul, Korea has not been successfully reproduced very many times in the United States. The reason for this is that churches have wanted the growth but have adopted *only a part* of the pattern of work and ministry values that have produced the kind of growth that has occurred in Seoul. With the exception of a handful of churches sparsely spread out across our land, there are few cell-group churches in the United States.

The Idea

Victor and Ruth Ann Martinez, directors of the Faith, Hope, and Love Center in El Carmen, Mexico introduced the original idea for cell groups to our senior pastor, Larry Stockstill. The Martinezes began a cell ministry in their church based on the cell concept used in El Salvador by Misión Cristiana Elim. This cell concept was one of evangelistic groups meeting twice a week, once for planning and once again for evangelism. Exposure to this concept birthed a stirring in Pastor Stockstill's heart. Our church already had small groups called "life groups," which met monthly for fellowship and Bible study. That was our way of satisfying the need of a few people in our congregation who felt that the church was too large to enjoy real fellowship and who needed closer contact with other believers. Many of these groups became such cliques, though, that the name "life group" became a misnomer. Sadly, they were *dead* as far as commitment to the purpose of reaching the lost.

A few months later, Pastor Mike Ware from Denver, Colorado, gave Dr. Ralph Neighbour's book, *Where Do We Go From Here?,* to Pastor Larry. Dr. Neighbour's philosophy of the cell church and his conviction is that the program-based church has failed in its attempt to evangelize the lost and effectively make disciples. While this was a bitter pill for someone who had been raised in such church patterns, it did serve as confirmation of how God was dealing with Pastor Larry. The reading of this book solidified Pastor Larry's direction. His stirring for evangelistic cell groups was confirmed, and his vision for cell-based ministry was enlarged.

Shortly thereafter, Pastor Larry met with the pastoral staff, explained to us how God was dealing with him about cell-based ministry, and shared his vision for implementing cell groups at Bethany. After much discussion concerning our structure of ministry, we realized that if we were going to start cells, it would require a total commitment from the entire staff. The only way to make cell ministry work was for it to become the **single** task of the church. It was imperative, therefore, that everyone be doing the same thing.

This represented a major change. Like most other churches, our church was divided into different programs with each staff member caring for his own area of responsibility. The church had many *parts*, but these parts did not fit together. Each program competed with the others for budget, volunteers, rooms, and attention from the pulpit. No matter how hard we tried to network, we couldn't seem to make the parts fit.

One example of the difficulty in meshing programs is what I experienced as the leader of the Follow-Up Team. Each week I would receive a number of altar cards that had been filled out by the people who had responded to the invitation to receive Christ either on Wednesday night or Sunday morning. On Tuesday nights I would meet with an average of twenty to thirty people and distribute the altar cards to the team. We would then phone each person, write a personal postcard, and try to make a visit to the person whose name was written on the card. The main purpose of the visit was to enroll the new believer in our Foundations Class for new Christians. While in the person's house, we also took the opportunity to share the Gospel with other members of the family and to pray with them.

After the person was enrolled in the Foundations Class, we would keep in contact with him/her for the seven-week period that the class lasted. I knew that each one of these new converts needed a place in the church body where he or she could be nurtured and discipled after finishing the class. We thought that we would be able to assimilate the new believers into our care-giving Life Groups, so I worked with the pastor in charge of that ministry to try to place the new converts into appropriate groups. To my amazement, none of the new believers were placed in a Life Group. As natural and simple an idea as it seemed, we were never able to come to an agreement with the Life Group leaders on how to implement the transition from one program to the other.

With two well-meaning pastors working together to merge the two ideas, we thought that the pieces would just fall together, but they didn't. We had some good ideas and tried to work out a mutually acceptable plan, but there was always a hitch somewhere that prevented the idea from becoming a reality. It just seemed impossible to get one program to **interface** with the other. I came to realize that we had two different visions trying to "hook-up" in mid-air; consequently, the plan was destined to fail.

With the decision to become a pure cell church, we realized that we were eventually going to have to transition out of all our old programs. To do that, we needed cooperation and synergy. Remember that synergy may be defined as the simultaneous action of different parts working together that creates an outcome greater than the sum of the individual parts. Synergy, however, does not occur in many local churches because there are too many different programs competing for attention. Since each program has its own identity and builds a wall around itself for survival, the local church ends up divided, with many entities that fail to cooperate with one another.

The Challenge of Growth

In 1992, we had approximately 2,800 to 3,000 people attending services on Sunday mornings. Although over 5,000 new people visited the church each year and hundreds responded to Christ at our altars, we were experiencing little growth. We did not have a net, an efficient means to assimilate all those visitors. We lacked a plan to involve our congregation in ongoing and effective ministry in the lives of the visitors and new converts. We did have faithful volunteers who came to nearly every church function and who were always on the verge of "burnout." For the rest of the congregation and for the incoming members, however, we offered only "pew" ministry: come, sit, and watch. As might be expected, this failed to produce the necessary interest level in people to lead them to become part of the church. We desperately wanted to open a door from our community into our church, but it just wasn't happening.

Although much of the congregation was getting "fat" on good spiritual food, they were not exercising their spiritual muscles in ministry. There was no church-wide vehicle for New Testament ministry that provided for the evangelizing of the lost and for the caring of the congregation's needs. I'm happy to report that in the seven years since starting cells, however, our church attendance has grown to over 6,000 in our weekend services, with over **600** cell groups actively meeting on a weekly basis. Why the big difference?

The Search for New Testament Ministry

Let me tell you how this happened. Faced with the glaring weaknesses of our program-based ministry and stirred by our exposure to cell-group ministry, we began our quest for information and training in cell ministry. You read in the last chapter about how, along with another pastor, I flew to San Salvador, El Salvador, to attend the Second International Seminar for Spiritual Leaders hosted by the senior pastor of the Misión Cristiana Elim. There we witnessed the motivation, the intensive labor, and the success of a cell-group church.

I marveled at the thousands of people (10,000 adults at a time, plus children) attending the eight Sunday services. The intensity of prayer, the worship, and the commitment of the Salvadorean people overwhelmed me. But the most moving aspect, as I shared in the previous chapter, was the humility of the leaders and the servant attitude they seemed to possess.

My life was changed in El Salvador. I knew that our vision for reaching our city could be accomplished if we could replicate the components of ministry that we were witnessing there. Subsequently, nearly all the Bethany staff pastors and several Bethany missionaries traveled to San Salvador to witness this ministry firsthand and to "catch" the vision. To a person, what we observed produced a hunger to see that kind of growth and commitment at Bethany for the lost.

Paving the Way for Cell-Group Ministry

Although what we observed in El Salvador was impressive, my new openness to ministry through cell groups was also the result of much prayer on the part of many people. The secret weapon, you see, will always be prayer—prayer that God initiates and obedient, hungry people are faithful to pray back to Him. Even before our introduction to cell ministry, God had prepared the way for us. Eighteen months before our visit to El Salvador, the Lord had led Pastor Stockstill to recruit and train a prayer army to intercede for the church and for our many missionaries around the world. Over 500 people responded and became a part of a weekly intercessory prayer group called Gideon's Army. The members of Gideon's Army went through twelve weeks of intensive prayer training with Suzette Hattingh's *Intercession as a Lifestyle* videos. (Hattingh leads an enormous group of intercessors for the Reinhard Bonnke Christ for All Nations ministry that has evangelized millions on the continent of Africa.) For the next year and a half, Gideon's Army consistently prayed for the church every Saturday morning, during Sunday services, and during the Wednesday night service.

When Pastor Stockstill decided it was time to implement cell groups, he started a ten-week training class on cell ministry for this very same Gideon's Army. The classes covered his vision for Bethany, the implementation of that plan, personal involvement of individuals, and church commitment to the concept. At the end of the initial training, 455 members of Gideon's Army were placed into 54 prayer cells, thus beginning the cell-group ministry at Bethany World Prayer Center.

Obstacles in the Way

Now we were going too far on the offensive, as far as the enemy was concerned. There were some stirrings and murmurings about the transition we planned to make. As with most churches who attempt this change, the initial obstacle to our church's acceptance of the cell concept was the old paradigm, or model, of program-based ministry. We realized that we had to shift away from this **program-based ministry to a people-based**

ministry, but the idea that cell groups would be the *basic unit of the church* instead of just an addendum to the existing church was a foreign concept to most of the congregation and the staff. Not everyone was willing to commit, and many had their faith challenged. However, as the pastors began to switch paradigms—and taught from the Bible on this model—the congregation caught the vision, and their commitment increased, along with their enthusiasm and motivation. They soon realized that cell ministry was the model most like New Testament ministry.

Over the next several months, we continued to train the cell leaders and their interns on various aspects of cell ministry. We taught them how to discover, develop, and deploy spiritual and ministry gifts, as well as teaching them basics about counseling and being good facilitators of cell group meetings. Since we were asking our new leaders to take positions on the "front line," we needed to give them the best training possible.

Several members of our staff, including myself, took trips to various successful cell-group churches around the world. We also attended cell seminars and conferences. We wanted to learn as much as possible from those who already had the experience in promoting cell ministry. Having caught the vision in El Salvador, our pastors were determined to implement that vision correctly. As we learned, we taught the congregation.

This didn't happen overnight. It was, in fact, over a forty-eight week period, through a cell leadership class on Wednesday nights, that we saw our leadership base expand. The *"equipping of the saints for the work of the ministry"* (Ephesians 4:12) was gradually becoming a reality at Bethany. Before the cell-group ministry, the saints were not involved in ministry because they were not equipped for it. **They were not equipped for ministry because there was no ministry in which they could become involved.** We had been a filling station, if you will, rather than an equipping station. But all that has changed. Today many members of Bethany are dynamic leaders in the church. They are the ones leading people to Christ, witnessing lives being changed, seeing the sick healed in their homes, and praying for revival in our city. These leaders are in the driver's seat of real New Testament ministry.

One main reason for this change is that the members of the cell-group ministry have caught the vision that **God can use them**. Previously, they just left all ministry to the pastoral staff because we did not have a vehicle for them to use. We could tell these leaders that God wanted to use them, but without a vehicle, the people just sat there. Through cell ministry, we have *created* ministry for the entire Body. We have helped the people move ministry to the needs of fellow believers and to the lost from the church into their homes.

It is so exciting to see the members at Bethany evangelizing the lost, caring for these new converts, and as under-shepherds, pastoring them effectively. The new converts are being exposed to the many benefits of a small-group setting, as well to the benefits of large congregational meetings. Now, when the pastor says, "Let's go," all these cell leaders lead their cell-group members with them in any direction the Lord might be leading. The congregation at Bethany has now become a mobilized army.

The Alternating Format

At Bethany, cell meetings are held every week, and the topic alternates between edification and evangelism, a principle we adopted from El Salvador. The edification meetings are designed for planning, prayer, and personal ministry. The evangelism meetings are designed for just that—to *evangelize*. Each cell member has the opportunity to bring a lost person to the evangelism meeting, and the topics planned for those meetings relate to a felt need, such as loneliness, fear, bitterness, addictions, family problems, and other relative subjects. This is an essential introduction that makes a connection in the mind of the lost person: "Come to our church; we can help meet your needs." At that point, these people stand in the receiving line and hungrily receive until they are saved and starting to grow in Christ. They could stay in this receiving mode for years, but as their needs become more sophisticated, the need for spiritual significance and purpose should be dealt with. This need cannot be met in the receiving line. At this point they must instead begin to experience the contribution line, a place where they are actually giving of themselves in some form of ministry to other people. Moving them from one mode to the next necessitates godly wisdom on the part of our cell leaders. Not a problem, as our God is faithful to supply all our needs according to His riches in Christ—especially wisdom. (See also James 1:5.)

Pulling Together

Getting back to our story, to keep pace with all the change and transition, the pastoral staff began to meet weekly for brainstorming, planning, and uniting vision. These team meetings promoted unity for the task at hand. As all the pastors began pulling together in the same direction to accomplish the same goals, our church seemed to take on new life and personality. Even our spiritual lives took on new dimensions. As cell-group ministry grew, vibrant people-based ministry replaced programs. As a staff, we were learning how to be a team working toward a common goal.

All the training, cell multiplication, and staff additions created the pressing need for district offices, resource materials, and report forms. Districts covering regional areas of the city were established. A district pastor supervised each district, and offices were set up in the back of the church for each district.

The cell groups were divided among the district offices according to geographical locations. All the forms were standardized, and resource materials were compiled and distributed. The cell ministry was broken into districts, zones, sections, and individual cells. Eventually, a 30,000 square foot addition to the church building was erected to accommodate the cell-group ministry. This Touch Center was dedicated November 13, 1994.

Cell groups are now the basis for every ministry in the church. If there is a death of a church member or his family member, the cell group in that area responds to the needs of that family. The zone pastors perform any weddings or funerals. Cell groups are assigned by zones to serve on Sundays as ushers, greeters, parking lot attendants, and nursery workers. Much of the day-to-day counseling is done by cell leaders within the zones. Only when a serious concern arises will a pastor be called for counseling assistance.

In the first eighteen months of cell ministry, the church grew by 1,500 people. To date, our Sunday attendance has grown from 2,800 to over 6,000. Presently we have over 600 cell groups, and over three thousand **new** people attend our weekend services. We are continuing to multiply cells, increase our leadership base, and learn more about maintaining the cell-church ministry. Finally, we have a net to hold the great catch.

Five Focus Points of Cell-Based Ministry

• **People** — Matthew 9:37-38: *"Then saith he unto his disciples, The harvest truly is plenteous, but the labourers are few; Pray ye therefore the Lord of the harvest, that he will send forth labourers into his harvest."*

While doing a seminar, I asked a local pastor, "In the light of the Great Commission, what percentage of your sermons do you preach to your congregation compared to unbelievers outside of your church building?" His answer would be typical of most pastors. He answered, "One hundred percent!"

I don't know about you, but that fact really disturbs me. If most of what we do is focused on the attendees of our Sunday services, how do we expect to grow from new converts? Recent studies show that eight-five percent of all churches in America are at a plateau or are declining in membership. Without a definite, Christ-centered strategy to win the lost, is it any wonder that so many churches are not experiencing conversion growth?

Let me share with you one additional principle we discovered—and this is exciting. The truth is that most of the leaders that you will need to grow your church, the money that you will need to build new buildings, and the people you will need to send missionaries are not in your church presently. **They are in the harvest!** Therefore, you must "feed the sheep," and focus on the harvest. *"Pray the Lord of the harvest to send out laborers into His harvest"* (Luke 10:2b, NKJV).

• **Process** — Our Leadership Base Path is the track that we put all new believers on to ensure that they have an opportunity to become leaders in the cell based church. Though they may not all finish the course, it is in place to put any person, regardless of their background experience or social position, where they can gain the skills to become effective for God in His Kingdom.

• **Structure** — The structure for governing and growing the cell groups is the "Principle of Twelve." It is a simple but highly effective way to raise up new believers and regular church members in tight-knit mentoring relationships. Proven to be a structure for rapid multiplication, the "Principle of Twelve" provides a strong foundation for discipleship and the care that small groups should offer. (This will be described in detail in Chapter 17).

• **Relationships** — Learning how to build strong relationships within family structures and within cell-group structures is extremely important to the success of the cell church.

You must learn how to change "metaphors" within the relationship. What I mean by this is demonstrated in successful parent/child relationships. For example, as a father I serve as teacher, a coach, a counselor, the judge, "executioner," and friend to my children. The mistake we make many times is to fail to change metaphors at the appropriate time. If I only relate to children as a teacher all the time, they will get tired of always getting instruction when they just need a friend to talk to. And it is the same with any metaphor; always a coach, always the judge, always the friend doesn't work.

A young father told me of a time when he went to coach his son on how to play baseball. He was trying to coach the boy on how to hit a ball. The child was not interested. It so angered the dad that his son was not being obedient, that he went from coach to judge and executioner! What started as a fun outing became a disciplinary event that could have had long-term negative results. Would the boy look forward to baseball with dad again? Not likely!

In the same way, we need to learn how to serve our cell-group members in a loving, non-judgmental way and learn to know what metaphor is needed in a given situation. Need a friend, a counselor, or a coach?

• **Lordship** — It is a mistake to think that we will ever occupy supreme authority over anyone in our groups. We can guide, advise, counsel and even correct when necessary, but we should never "lord it over" anyone. People are free to choose their own direction for their lives under the exclusive lordship of Christ.

The lordship of Jesus Christ becomes the motivating force that causes any member of the Body of Christ to "take up his cross" and follow Jesus. When lordship under Christ is perfectly understood and properly responded to, the Christian will loving and eagerly follow all that God wants him to do. There is no coercion on our part as leaders that can substitute for the submission of the individual to His Lord's commands. Rather than attempting to control and direct in every instance, we should live to protect the individual's right to respond to the sovereignty of Jesus' lordship over his/her life.

Book of Acts Ministry

The idea to implement cell-group ministry at Bethany took courage and a willingness to abandon three decades of a ministry style. The implementation of that vision, however, has totally revolutionized our understanding of New Testament ministry. The decision to become a cell church has transformed the entire church from a "come-and-see" mentality to a "go-and-show" mentality. Truly God has honored this step toward a book of Acts style of ministry as we have moved from programs to people.

Chapter 3

Winds of Change

I enjoy hearing stories and I love to tell stories—especially humorous ones that illustrate a point I'm trying to make. Here's one that applies to many of the transitional situations we have faced. It's one of my Cajun stories about a character I call Boudreaux.

Boudreaux lived in South Louisiana and was a fur trapper by trade, just like his relatives who had come here in the mid 1700s from Nova Scotia. When Boudreaux brought his furs to sell to the buyers one day, the buyer gave him a check. Now, banks had just moved into the South Louisiana area, and he had never seen a check. Boudreaux said, "Whass dat?"

The buyer said, "That's a check. Just take that to the bank and they will give you your money."

Boudreaux said, "I like dat."

So Boudreaux went to the bank and gave the banker the check. The banker said, "Fine. Please endorse it."

Boudreaux said, "Endorse, whass dat?"

The banker said, "Sign the back of the check and I will give you the money."

Boudreaux said, "The man told me to give you the check and you'd give me the money. I ain't signin' nuttin!"

The banker said, "Boudreaux, if you don't sign the check, we can't give you the money."

Boudreaux said again, "I ain't signin' nuttin!" And he took his check and went down to the next bank.

He walked into the next bank and said to the banker there, "Here's my check. Gimme the money."

The banker said, "Fine, Boudreaux. Just sign the check and I'll give you the money."

Boudreaux said, "I ain't signin' nuttin!"

The banker answered, "Boudreaux, you gotta sign the check before I can give you the money."

Boudreaux repeated, "I ain't sigin' nuttin. The man told me t'give you the check and you'd give me the money."

The banker lost his temper, grabbed Boudreaux and slapped him five times. Then he said, "Sign the check, Boudreaux!"

Boudreaux said, "No problem," and he signed the check and got his money.

On the way back to his boat, Boudreaux stopped by the first bank and waved the money at the first banker. He said, "Look here, I got my money!"

The banker asked, "Did you sign the check?"

Boudreaux said, "Yes."

The banker said, "Boudreaux, I told you that if you would sign the check, I would've given you the money."

Boudreaux replied, "Yeah, you told me, but you didn't splain it to me like dat utter man did!"

I'm not advocating violence, but I think you get the point. Effective communication is a key element when experiencing change, wouldn't you agree? Because of the high regard with which the congregation at Bethany held Pastor Larry Stockstill, our move to cell-based ministry was not as difficult a transition as faces many churches where there is a credibility gap. Of course, we still had obstacles to climb, old paradigm ministry dogmas to overcome, and a void of experience in the cell-church model. There were pastors who had poured their lives into certain program-based ministries that found it difficult to abandon the old programs. One pastor would grimace every time we would ask him when he was going to discontinue his meetings with the old program. He finally took courage and closed it down. Today, he is glad he did. Some congregational members had strong attachments to the programs that they participated in because of relationships with other people in those same programs. And as expected, others just found it hard to accept change. The Holy Spirit, however, led us ever so specifically as we sought Him for guidance in providing the best possible pastoral care for His sheep.

We learned in the process of the transition how to train our leaders to take over the responsibilities of each of the programs that we were discontinuing, only in a cell-group context. This gave most everyone a confidence that no one would be left behind in the process and that the vital ministry functions of each program would be carried over into the cells in an effective manner.

Before cells, Bethany was not overly organized in church programs, but we did have our share. The transition out of these programs was immediate for some, such as the follow-up team, but was very slow and careful for others, such as the alcohol and drug rehabilitation ministry. Traditional programs, such as the singles ministry and youth group, were easy to transition into cells. Others, such as the Lifeline telephone ministry that maintained twenty-four hour call-in prayer, took more time to transition. With the transition into cell-based ministry nearly complete at Bethany, we are now beginning to appreciate the dynamic of having over six hundred leaders across our city leading three thousand people each week in life-changing ministry.

An Exciting Challenge

Transitioning to the cell-church concept has been an exciting time for the church. Bethany broke out of a mold that was successful by normal church standards and instead entered into the book of Acts model that had the potential to "turn the world upside down." It was a major change for all on staff and for the congregation. Excitement, apprehension, and a sense of challenge filled the emotions of everyone involved.

It was in early April 1993 that we birthed those first fifty-four prayer cells with four hundred fifty-five members from our Gideon's Army intercessory prayer team. By the first week of October in that year, the original fifty-four groups had multiplied to one hundred and eight groups. We had begun a leadership class back in April and it, too, was in full swing, training the original as well as the new, emerging leaders. Our focus was to inspire, instruct, and motivate the leaders with vision.

At this point, the cell concept was so new and unpredictable that each day brought with it new revelations concerning the challenges of the cell church. Learning to handle our growth successfully and keeping everyone motivated and trained made this journey both challenging and exciting. By our first anniversary, April 1994, we had multiplied to two hundred and sixteen groups. God had given us success, but we were not ready to declare the victory yet. Our goal was to reach the city, not just to have lots of groups.

Critical Mass

The six-month multiplication cycle began to markedly decrease as we approached "critical mass." The number of groups and group members was catching up with the original size of our congregation, and leaders were more and more difficult to find. If there was one weakness in our structure that was beginning to show, it was the absence of a proven leadership track that would provide upward mobility for future leaders. Although we were still conducting the leadership class, there was no practical leadership training on the cell-group level.

After months of research and just plain old searching, we came up with our Leadership Discipleship Track (LDT). It combined practical leadership training with the discipleship of new believers being done by cell-group members. LDT was the beginning and not the end of an effective process for training leaders to accommodate future growth. We have since replaced LDT with a process for discipleship and development of leaders that includes the same concepts but is easier to employ. We call this system the "Leadership Base Path." This system was employed as a practical way of carrying out our vision statement. "Bethany World Prayer Center exists to preach the Gospel to every person, pastor believers, prepare disciples and plant leaders around the world." This process verifies the new believer's salvation and then assimilates him into the cell- group ministry as well as into the local church celebration services. With the goal of making leaders out of every new convert, the system brings people through the necessary classes for foundational Bible truths and leadership skills that will help them become successful when they actually start leading a cell group. The process is defined more thoroughly in Chapter 13, "Components of the Cell Group."

As cell groups began to increase, so did the need for additional staff to oversee the expanding number of groups and cell members. Over the first two and one-half years, we added twelve new zone pastors to oversee the growing number of cell groups. Along with the addition of pastors who came up through the ranks at Bethany, we also added support staff, such as secretaries and administrative personnel. To physically accommodate the increasing number of staff members, we broke ground and completed a new building called the Touch Center.

The results of cell-group ministry have been nothing less than miraculous. The church has grown in every way: spiritually, numerically, in ministry, and financially. In six years we have grown from 2700 giving families to over 5800 giving families, but more importantly, we have grown in the area of pastoral care. Evangelism has increased dramatically as well. **Within the first five years we had 5000 souls come to Christ in cell groups**. For the first time in my twenty years of ministry, I feel confident that when a person approaches the church with a need, regardless of its dimension, we can now meet that need effectively. It is a great comfort to know that instead of only a few overworked pastors, we now have a trained army of over six hundred experienced leaders who are ready to accept the challenge of ministry.

The Change Process

"I have to let go of what I have in order to grasp something else."
"Letting go of the old is the first step in grasping the new."

You might ask, "So, how do we get there from here?" Good question. As I look back at how the Lord led us in the transition, I see **several key elements that were necessary to make the transition successfully.** In Chapter 6, "How to Transition," we will discuss the details. Here I would like to introduce the principles that I think helped us in the process.

- **The Mandate - Create a Sense of Urgency** — "There's coming a harvest and a hostility, and you are not ready for either." This is the statement the Lord spoke to Pastor Larry Stockstill that created the urgency in his heart to change the way we did things at Bethany. Without urgency, it is difficult to move people from complacency. Let's face it, church is good! Worship is great, the preaching is moving, and most of my needs are met. So, why rock the boat? Believe me, without a sense of urgency you will be fighting an uphill battle to get people excited about the transition to cell church.

Two things help create that sense of urgency. 1.) Communicating the mandate and emphasizing the potential catastrophes. "If we don't make this change, we will miss out on the harvest that the Lord wants to send." Or, "We have not provided the members of this congregation with a meaningful ministry opportunity and therefore have not addressed their need for purpose." 2.) Recognizing the opportunities that change will help the church capitalize on in regard to souls, and identifying the potential positive benefits available to each member if the change is made (i.e., more training in personal ministry, recapturing the home for Christ, more fulfillment in their Christian walk, better care for the new believers, etc.).

- **A Strong Transition Team - A Change Coalition** — In December of 1991, our pastoral staff went on a retreat where a seminar was given entitled "Team Management." This helped set the stage for what would be our "Transition Team" for cells. A little over one year later, in early 1993, Pastor Larry Stockstill designated a "Cell Coordinator," District Pastors, and Zone Pastors with the existing staff. This group met weekly for the next three years overseeing the transition process. To this day, this team continues to meet to discuss necessary changes in structure, troubleshoot problems, and brainstorm over new ideas. Without a strong team, I am convinced that we would have given into the ministry culture that was present in the church then and would have changed very little, if at all.

In his book *Leading Change*, John Kotter calls this group the "guiding coalition."[1] Just like our military coalition with other nations when we fought in Iraq and Kosovo, the coalition must stay intact for the duration of the process. Had any nation in the NATO coalition pulled out, it would have caused much confusion and hardship for all other nations involved. In the church, this coalition must be made up of the Senior Pastor, and **all** key staff persons. Otherwise, in times of challenge, many may question the wisdom of various new policies and of the Holy Spirit's leading in the new endeavor. Even with this strong team, you may face opposition from well-meaning associates who find it difficult to let go of the old paradigm. The best thing to do is to keep them in the process, and bring them up to your level of understanding of both the mandate and the information that you have. Eventually every person on staff will either accept the change or leave. As with most organizations, it is sometimes necessary to replace staff in order to bring about necessary changes. The Lord knows your heart and desire and will surely help you in that process.

- **A Clear Vision - Write it Down** — In the church in El Salvador nearly every member could quote from memory the vision of Misión Cristiana Elim. Here it is: "I have a purpose. My purpose is to win souls. I can best fulfill my purpose in a group. I will not be happy until I have fulfilled my

---

[1] See page 6 of this excellent book. (Harvard Business School Press, 1996).

purpose. I have no promise of tomorrow." The leadership team should hammer out a simple but thorough vision statement that every person in the congregation can repeat from memory.

The statement that we eventually came up with is this: "Bethany World Prayer Center exists to preach the Gospel to every creature, pastor believers, prepare disciples, and plant leaders around the world." It is simple, yet complete. A simple statement may take time to produce, and may change as time goes on (ours did), but work on it until it says what you want it to say. You may also take it a step further by adding as an addendum your goals, strategy, and plans for accomplishing the vision. Then, whatever you have to do to get the word out, do it to every level of the church organization and community. Every person should communicate the vision repeatedly until it has permeated the entire church.

Vision Multiplied by 1000! Every vision must be communicated over and over again for it to become part of the organization's life-blood. For example, if the pastor shares the vision for cells every Sunday for the entire year, that's 52 times the most important aspect of your future ministry is talked about. However, if 100 cell members and leaders each tell 10 people per week about what God is doing in cells, that's 52,000 times per year that the vision is shared. This was the case at Bethany and the reason we had such motivation in the starting of the cell ministry.

- **Equip the Masses - Every Person Is a Potential Leader** — To make sure that the change is completed, you will have to train and retrain your staff and congregational leaders in the new disciplines of the cell-church structure. Because of the scope of cell-group leadership, the average Christian in our churches does not have all the skills to carry on long-term effective ministry. You should prepare for ongoing training that will add to each person the skills that any pastor or staff member would be required to have. The only exception would be formal theological training in a college or university setting. It is not necessary to have that broad a background. However, they should be trained in doctrine, your statement of faith, evangelism, counseling, and how to effectively lead others in a small-group setting. Other skills necessary include how to do a successful follow-up visit, how to minister to the sick, and how to make effective telephone follow-up calls.

Remember, if people are asked to do tasks that they are not equipped to do, they will eventually drop out. It is imperative that you constantly get feedback from the leaders on the possible training that they feel they need and then provide it. When training breaks down, the change process will slow down. Also, it is always wise to have leaders repeat "basic training" if their cell groups begin to flounder. Most often the group fails because of the little mistakes that are made or when simple items in the structure are forgotten or overlooked.

- **Have Short-Term Wins Along the Way - Morale Boosters** — Any endeavor can lose its appeal, and excitement can wane if there is not obvious progress soon after you begin. One of the great morale boosters that kept the fires burning in our cell-church transition was the incremental growth that occurred on a weekly basis. This kept the cell leaders and members motivated, and still does. Every time someone would suggest that cell groups could not work in the U.S., I just quoted directly from the Coordinator's Report the results of growth that we had experienced. Eventually, nearly everyone accepted the cell-church structure and supported the change effort.

One danger that exists is declaring victory too soon. On page 12 of *Leading Change*, John Kotter says, "While celebrating a win is fine, any suggestion that the job is mostly done is generally a terrible mistake." Until the change has become "organic" and is a normal part of the new culture, you can destroy the sense of urgency by declaring, "We did it!" too soon. Soldiers who come off of the front lines with a sense of having won the war are very hard to convince that they need to re-enlist for another tour of duty.

- **Know that Change is Here to Stay - Don't Stop Changing**

The chance for growth requires the risk of change.

Change can cause a sense of instability, but not continuing to change can undo all the changes that you made to get where you are. When we reached the three hundred mark in the number of family-type cell groups, our growth slowed to a screeching halt. Why? Because we had assimilated most of the people in our congregation who wanted to be in cells, along with their family members and friends, and simply ran out of people to bring in. It was necessary to change direction and

begin our homogeneous cells in workplaces and among special interest groups in order to be exposed to more people that we could eventually reach for Christ. Hundreds of groups were birthed and we began to
grow again.

Just as during the Industrial Age, the Space Age, and the Computer
Age, change caused temporary instability for many of us, yet these
changes have been for our good. The same is true for the changes that
you will make to transition into cells, even if it causes temporary dis-
comfort. When your cell growth slows down, don't be afraid to introduce
new follow-up plans or evangelism outreaches. It will cause a stir perhaps, but a stir is what most of us need from time to time. Just make
sure that the changes reach a completion stage and are part of the
structure before changing the changes!

Change the Destiny of Your Church

While some churches do provide meaningful participation in ministry
within their structure, many, if not most, do not. Therefore, it is important
to communicate to the leadership and congregation the absolute necessity of change. Learn all that you can about managing transitions and gain
the necessary skills to see the change come to its final and successful
conclusion. The change in vision and structure at Bethany World Prayer
Center has changed our destiny. We are now entering our seventh year
of cell-based ministry and are committed to pressing forward with the vision. As we proceed, we are learning what changes need to take place
and are fine-tuning our leadership-training materials. These materials are
being made available through our office to church leaders around the
world who have embraced the cell-church model of ministry.

Thousands of church leaders across America and other parts of the
globe have come to our cell conferences to receive training in cell-based
ministry. In addition, many members of our pastoral staff travel around
the country holding seminars for interested churches. By God's grace,
our next goal is to have one thousand cell groups in the Baton Rouge
area that are effectively ministering to between ten and fifteen thousand
people.

Chapter 4

Why Cells?

Sam Lesky's Personal Testimony

My wife, Joan, and I have been married for twelve years, and we have two daughters, ages 8 and 11. The first six years of our marriage, we were not committed Christians, and we found ourselves struggling to keep our marriage together. We had problems with finances, drugs, alcohol and a lack of sexual intimacy. We weren't happy or peaceful; we knew something was missing. We had a religious knowledge of Jesus, but were not committed in following the ways of the Lord.

When God came into the picture, life would never be the same.

It all started when my wife was approached at the playground and asked to attend a women's small group. My wife was anxious to meet people, and figured that hearing a little about God couldn't hurt her. When she went to the small group, they were teaching about how to be a Christian wife.

During this time I was actively using drugs and alcohol and was definitely focused on a materialistic world. As time went by, my wife committed her life to Christ and became filled with the Holy Spirit and brought prayer into our home. Then the same woman who invited my wife to the cell-group meeting invited me to church to hear the worship. I went to the service and could not believe how much fun it was to worship God. Then the big moment came when my wife approached me about going to a small group on a Friday night with her. Friday nights were for partying downtown, not hanging out with a bunch of 'Bible geeks.'

At the same time I was having pain in my shoulder from a college football injury. I knew my wife had her prayer time and believed strongly in God's power, and I was somewhat irritated about her being caught up in God. I made a bet with her that if she prayed and my shoulder was healed I would go "once" to the cell group. She took me up on it and prayed for me that night. After a couple of days I noticed the pain in my shoulder was gone, but of course I was not going to admit that right away. A few days later I finally told her what happened. I had committed to attend one small-group meeting. I will never forget walking into that house on a Friday night. As I looked at the counter at the refreshments all I saw was soft drinks, no alcohol. We made it through the whole meeting and I was quite amazed that these normal guys could go without drinking, using drugs or cursing. Several of the men reached out to me, and we developed a relationship. I got to experience firsthand men walking out their Christian beliefs. It was through this group that I learned not only God's word, but also how to have a personal relationship with the Lord. I began to attend church regularly and then worked on not cursing, and on giving up drugs and alcohol. God kept drawing me closer and closer to Him, and I began to realize true peace and joy were from the Lord, not the world. We have more fun and laugh more now then we ever did. Praise God for cell groups and the accountability we have to one another!

Our Future Is the Past

It seems that the Bible rewrites itself every time the Church discovers some new idea from it that causes growth or sends some form of help that we haven't had before. God's word is eternal but also contemporary. The "house-to-house" ministry of the book of Acts seems to have been hidden from most of us until recent years, but now it is illuminated before our eyes. How could we not have seen the explosive results of thousands of new believers meeting together daily to break bread and preach Christ? Why didn't we realize that these house meetings were with people with whom the new convert had a close relationship, and that the growth of the Early Church was through the evangelization of these relationships? We would have failed the test before, but now we see. Why cells rather than another program-based method? Let's look and see.

A Basic Unit

When church leadership is confronted with the concept of cell groups, the first question is "Why cells?" The answer is best explained by using the example of living cells in the human body. Cells are the basic unit of life, and all further life develops through the multiplication of those cells. Each cell of the body possesses its own unique makeup. Many genetic diseases and even deaths result from the absence of, or a deficiency in, a particular enzyme or DNA strand within the cell itself. Where there are deficiencies, there can be no ongoing life. Simply stated, if the cells of the human body are healthy, the entire body is healthy. If the cells are sick, the body is sick. The church, like the human body, must be composed of healthy cells if the whole body is to be healthy.

The **traditional, program-based local church** is composed of a mixture of programs started as a result of the latest idea passed down by a visiting pastor or evangelist. There is no real strategy involved, no basic unit by which to measure the whole. The church is simply the product of an evolution of years of ideas that have been passed down without ever considering the bigger picture. Many of these programs have been out of touch with the needs of the local assembly for some time but have taken on a life of their own. Because of the committed volunteers, annual budgets, and the feeling that the members need to be involved, the programs continue year after year, *regardless of the success of the program*.

A good example of this was illustrated in a major city by a church that had a counseling center located approximately twenty-five miles from the church. There was a staff pastor assigned to it and a budget of over $70,000 a year allocated to it, but it had no actual place in the daily operation of the local church. I asked the pastor two questions. I wanted to know if there were any souls won at the counseling center, or better yet, if anyone had been added to the local church as a result of the center's ministry within the past few months. His answer was "no" to both questions.

If measured by any other commercial standard of efficiency and returns on investment of time and personnel, this church program, like most church programs, would rate very poorly. But because many programs in the local church practically become institutions, the local church just keeps renewing their budgets, thus perpetuating their life expectancies indefinitely. As a result, languishing programs continue year after year, unnoticed and unproductive.

Our experience has been that the **cell church** is the most efficient means of reaching unbelievers and pastoring believers. Because the cell groups are given responsibility for all aspects of local church ministry, except for Sunday celebration services, close accountability exists, and productivity is easily measured. If an individual cell is unproductive, the leadership of that cell is changed, or the group is assimilated into another more productive group, or special attention is given to the ailing cell until it regains its health. By carefully monitoring the health of the individual cells, the cell church thus avoids the continuation of dead programs or traditions that have outlived their usefulness.

Dynamics of the Early Church

The book of Acts reveals that the early church possessed all the components necessary to maintain spiritual power and to experience growth in the Kingdom of God. This was accomplished at both temple and house meetings. *"So continuing daily with one accord in the temple, and breaking bread from house to house, they ate their food with gladness and simplicity of heart"* (Acts 2:46, NKJV). *"And daily in the temple, and in every house, they did not cease teaching and preaching Jesus as the Christ"* (Acts 5:42, NKJV). All church business, spiritual and otherwise, was taken care of in these home meetings. Paul's letters were read not only to the believers in the temple, but also to those in the homes where the church met.

The church today cannot survive without the same dynamics found in the Early Church. In Acts 19:23, the Bible declares that what the apostles did through this kind of home ministry caused *"no small stir."* I've often asked myself the question, "When has my ministry caused *'no small stir'*? When have I stirred up anything in my community for the sake of Christ?" In Acts 17:6, the Bible states that the city elders accused the apostles of *"turning the world upside down."* With God's grace, we can still turn the world upside down.

As we investigate the Early Church's ministry activities, we discover the immense influence wielded by the church through house-to-house ministry. In Acts 8:5-8, the Bible describes Philip's going into a city, preaching there, and then the whole city responding to his message. There was *"great rejoicing in the city."* Why? The city accepted Jesus! My desire is to one day see *"great rejoicing in* [my] *city"* over Jesus. Such things will happen, however, only when we return to powerful New Testament Christianity. I believe that the best example of New Testament Christianity to be found today is cell-group ministry.

A Microcosm of the Kingdom

When I started studying "cell groups" in the New Testament, I read the book of Acts over and over again. Those little churches that met in believers' homes did not just have fellowship. They had it all! In a meeting, a person could receive whatever he needed, whether it be salvation, deliverance from demons, healing, training in the Word, or discipling. Active participation in the ministry that followed belonged to everyone. All the activities of the church occurred at the meetings in the believers' homes. There was nothing lacking. This is spelled out in I Corinthians 14:26. *"How is it then, brethren? Whenever you come together, each of you has a psalm, has a teaching, has a tongue, has a revelation, has an interpretation. Let all things be done for edification"* (NKJV).

A cell group differs from a **small group** in that a small group has a single focus dealing with only one area of need, whereas **a cell group is a microcosm** of the Kingdom of God. By that I mean that within a cell group exist all the components of the Kingdom, with the most basic being to love thy neighbor as thyself. Let me explain it this way. I live in South Louisiana near the Gulf of Mexico. If I went out to the Gulf of Mexico, scooped up a bucketful of water, and tasted it, the water would taste salty. If I emptied that bucket and then filled it with pure drinking water, sprinkled salt in it, and tasted the water, it, too, would taste salty. Both buckets of water may taste the same and look the same, but they are entirely different. The bucket with water from the Gulf contains all the salts, dissolved gasses, and organic substances that are found in the Gulf, whereas the other contains only salt and water. Although the water from both buckets looks and tastes the same, the bucket with only salt does not possess all the macro- and micro-nutrients found in the bucket with water taken from the Gulf. The water of the Gulf of Mexico can sustain a broad spectrum of sea life, both animal and plant, but the salt water that was artificially created cannot sustain life.

The church with program-type small groups is often like this second bucket. It may have groups that meet for fellowship, for prayer, for Bible study, or even for evangelism, and it may look like the "real thing." It may offer a variety of programs, but each program stands alone and offers only a limited scope of ministry. Programs in such a church are normally *single-faceted ministries* that are confined to the *definition of the program.* Program-based small-group ministries are nearly always limited in the same way. These groups are small groups, but they are not cell groups. They are limited in scope, in vision, and in ministry. They do not have all the necessary components for sustaining life; consequently, most such groups and programs, even the very best and most enjoyable ones, have limited life spans.

On the other hand, the bucket with the water from the Gulf of Mexico includes every necessary component. It can sustain an abundance of sea life, *just as a cell group sustains church life.* The gasses, organic substances, and minerals in the water are conducive to reproduction. This bucket of water is a microcosm of the Gulf of Mexico, just as a cell group is a microcosm of the Kingdom of God. In every cell group, people can be evangelized, receive prayer, healing, deliverance, fellowship, Bible teaching, edification, visitation, follow-up, discipleship, and more. Anything needed in the Body of Christ ought to be found in the cell group. This may sound like an overwhelming task, yet I'm here to witness that—by God's grace—it is entirely possible. We work continually to maintain this broad spectrum of ministry in each of our cell groups. Some of these individual components of cell ministry are discussed below.

Recapturing Families

As believers, we do not realize our true spiritual condition until we are challenged to come out from our comfort zones. After their involvement in cell-group ministry, several of our cell leaders have remarked how much closer to Christ the experience had brought them.

When believers get involved in ministry, they move out of the receiving mode and into the giving mode, out of the distribution line and into the contribution line.[1] When they begin using their homes to host cell-group meetings, they bring ministry activity right into the heart of their lives and are actually touching lives all around them, just as Jesus commanded. The most important thing that happens to those who become involved in cell ministry is that *they recapture their own homes.* Instead of Little League, television, and Nintendo dominating their lives, the cell group and the resultant ministry to the Lord and to people become the central focus. There is still time for fun and games, but the lives of the believers are not consumed with such things anymore.

---

[1] Concept drawn from William Beckham, *The Second Reformation,* TOUCH Publications, 1995.

In the cell-group ministry, parents live out the love of Christ in front of their children. As a result, the children, too, are often involved in ministry and serving God. One lady, telling me the effect that cell groups had made in her home life, said, "We used to go to church to get God and bring Him home. Now we get God at home and bring Him to church!"

Testimony of Pastor Charles Lambert, Tustin, California

The growth that has resulted from our transition has gone beyond my greatest expectations. We began a year ago with 20 cells. For years we could not break the attendance barrier of 110 people for our mid-week service and programs. However, since January of 2000 we now consistently average over 170 people throughout the week in cells. Our Wednesday night youth service could not break the 20-25 attendance barrier but now, our weekly youth cells are averaging over 35 youth.

*Through cell evangelism, **my church has reached nearly fifty families** who had no previous relationship with us. I am also excited because **three people have made personal decisions to follow Jesus Christ in the past three months.***

My belief in cell ministry has not just been influenced by increased numbers. I have seen family after family touched by God's presence and power. We have adopted the philosophy that 'cells are wells.' They have become a place where our people gather to reach God and to reach out to others.

Satisfying the Hungry and Thirsty Heart

God is in the business of changing people. Christians are not satisfied or changed without encountering the very presence of God. Once they have been in His presence, they are not satisfied with just having Bible study or fellowship groups. They want every mighty ingredient of the Gospel to be present in their lives, including the power of God.

Ministry was never intended to work without God's power. Structure may be necessary, but if the structure doesn't receive power, it won't be life producing, and the structure alone will not sustain ministry. We need every powerful element of the Gospel of Christ working in our lives on a consistent basis. Cell-group ministry helps to provide Christians with access to every element.

Why is the power of God moving today? I believe it is because Christians are getting _connected._ Two outpourings of the Holy Spirit that really demonstrate the power in such unity occurred on the day of Pentecost (Acts 2:1-4) and in the church of Antioch (Acts 13:1-2). In the first event, the 120 were all together in one place, in one accord, and they were worshipping God. The Bible says that the Spirit of God fell powerfully on them with tongues of fire and the sound of a mighty rushing wind. In the second event at the church in Antioch, the believers were worshipping and ministering to the Lord. Again, the Spirit of God fell in a powerful way. When the Holy Spirit fell in these two instances, dynamic ministry was imparted. The same type of power is definitely needed in the church today. Through cell-group ministry, the demonstration of such power becomes a reality as believers connect by worshipping God in one accord, with one vision; and He, in turn, visits them.

It is the anointing of God that breaks the yoke of bondage in people's lives. _"And it shall come to pass in that day, that his burden shall be taken away from off thy shoulder, and his yoke from off thy neck, and the yoke shall be destroyed because of the anointing"_ (Isaiah 10:27). When believers come together to worship and pray, they should expect the Holy Spirit to do something. This innate desire for interaction with a powerful God and His people is satisfied in the cell-group ministry. In the cell group, the yearning to be used and fulfilled is realized as individuals are given opportunity to be all that God intended them to be in an environment where God can be all that He desires to be. Contrast this with what is often an American tradition, the spectator worship service.

We'll learn more about cell-group interaction in the chapter on mentoring.

Increasing the Church

Christian Schwarz, author of _Natural Church Development,_ studied over 100 churches in 32 countries on all five inhabited continents. On page 33 of his book he states, "If we were to identify any one principle as the 'most important,' then, without a doubt, it would be the multiplication of small groups." Such a statement is borne out by the fact that the largest churches in the world today are cell-group churches. Yoido Full Gospel Church in Seoul, Korea; Misión Cristiana Elim in San Salvador, El Salvador;

and Misión Carismática Internacional in Bogotá, Colombia are all fast-growing churches with memberships numbering 100,000 or more. There are other cell churches in Manila, Philippines, and in Abijan, Ivory Coast, West Africa, as well as in many other cities around the world. These churches all have memberships in the tens of thousands. Surely the harvest is being gathered in these churches.

I want to take a moment to talk about the harvest as a metaphor. Sometimes I don't know how to get people passionate about the harvest except to look at the importance of the harvest to the people of the Old and New Testament times. The harvest was their very life. Without the harvest, they could not eat or pay their bills. They'd actually go into a form of servant bondage without the harvest. Does this give a clearer picture of how absolutely vital the harvest would be to Jesus' audience? *"Do you not say, 'There are still four months and then comes the harvest'? Behold, I say to you, lift up your eyes and look at the fields, for they are already white for harvest!"* (John 4:35, NKJV). The word Jesus used for *look* is an advanced stage of looking in which there is a total commitment, a willingness to forsake all for the thing you are looking at. This is certainly not just a casual glimpse.

Please remember that without a harvest, your church can't grow. All your future leaders are out there in the harvest.

Exercising of Spiritual Gifts

I Corinthians 14:26 says, *"How is it then, brethren? When ye come together, every one of you hath a psalm, hath a doctrine, hath a tongue, hath a revelation, hath an interpretation. Let all things be done unto edifying."*

Once again, one of the most obvious Scriptures that is impossible to fulfill in a Sunday morning service is the above-quoted verse, I Corinthians 14:26. Even with a small congregation of fifty, people would need to spend hours taking turns exercising their gifts, as described in this Scripture. In a small group of eight or ten people, however, this can be easily accomplished to the edification of the entire group.

Testimony of Reverend C. D. Murray, Elkton, Maryland

The gifts of the Spirit are a normal part of our church services, and continue to operate in the cells. ... Relationships are developing and personal needs are being ministered to and met in a great way. Individuals who were never involved are getting involved and showing interest that was not evidenced before. Reports of healing, deliverance, and salvation are being reported. Our plans are to move forward in faith under the direction of the Holy Spirit. Our expectations are great for the future. Our vision is clear... souls, growth. Our excitement is overwhelming...

Making Disciples

Matthew 28:19 (Darby) says, *"Go [therefore] and make disciples of all the nations, baptizing them to the name of the Father, and of the Son, and of the Holy Spirit."*

The New Testament model of "making disciples" goes far beyond the ability of the best Sunday morning service. Even with Sunday School and other training classes, there remains a void of daily, ongoing, face-to-face contact of the type that Jesus modeled to His own disciples, with constant real-life, practical examples of the way we should live as Christians. In fact, to make disciples in the Hebrew sense of the term is to live the life of a mentor before your protégé. Intimate relationships cannot be nurtured in large gatherings but are more successfully attained in the setting of a cell group. Even then, the effort to connect with others and provide oversight and training is a great challenge. (Chapters 16 and 17, "Mentoring" and "The Principle of Twelve and Multiplication" will share procedures that assist in meeting this challenge.)

Having True Fellowship and Edification

Ephesians 4:15-16 states, *"But speaking the truth in love, may grow up into him in all things, which is the head, [even] Christ. From whom the whole body fitly joined together and compacted by that which every joint supplieth, according to the effectual working in the measure of every part, maketh increase of the body unto the edifying of itself in love."*

In our Sunday services we experience many great dynamics of corporate worship, such as the preaching of the Word and the sense of belonging to the bigger work of God. But it would be stretching it to say that we have fellowship one with another. It would be even more of an overstatement to say that we *"fitly join together and that every joint supplies accord-*

ing to the effectual working in the measure of every part." We have cordial greetings and we chat, but we do not have much in the way of true Christian fellowship on Sunday morning. Sunday mornings are just not designed for that deep sharing or intense dialogue. The cell group, however, is custom-made for its members to fitly join together and share the measure of Christ that is given to each member. As the group grows in love and accountability, growth and maturity will be the result.

Chapter 5

Components of a Successful Cell Church

On their first ever airplane flight, Boudreaux and Thibodeaux were on their way to New York. A few minutes after takeoff, there was a loud noise from outside the plane. Momentarily, the pilot came on the address system and said, "Ladies and gentlemen, I know that you heard that loud noise. We have just lost an engine. But don't worry about it at all. We still have three very strong jet engines left...however, we will be about an hour late as a result of losing that engine."

About thirty minutes later, another loud noise was heard. The pilot came back on the address system and said, "Ladies and gentlemen, I am sure that you heard that loud noise. We have lost another engine, but don't worry, we have two very strong engines left...however, that will make us about two hours late!"

Again, within a few minutes, a third loud noise was heard and the pilot came back on to speak to the passengers. "Ladies and gentlemen, don't be alarmed at that noise. We have lost another engine, but we still have one very, very strong engine left. However, that will make us three hours late."

Boudreaux then looked at Thibodeaux and said, "Thibodeaux, if that last engine goes out, we gonna be up here all day!"

The fact that Boudreaux often comes to absurd conclusions is what makes these stories so entertaining. But in real life, we want to consider all our data very carefully before making decisions.

Pastors often ask me, "Do you think that we can transition to a cell-group church?" My immediate answer often is "That depends on a number of major issues!" Starting a cell-group church is not something a pastor decides to do just because he would like to see growth in his church or wants more tithers and fewer counseling responsibilities. The first and foremost reason to transition to a cell-group church is that such a church is Biblical, both from Scriptural examples and from the development of the personality of Jesus. Thus, before beginning the transition process, there must be an inner conviction of the heart, a "do it or die" commitment to becoming a biblically based cell church.

There must also be the right type of foundation in place to ensure success. To begin with, character and spiritual fortitude are always prerequisites to success in ministry of any kind. In addition, many churches will need to correct the prevailing problem of a governmental structure that can be fatal to cell-group ministry. In those cases, the church must make sure that the governmental structure is realigned to allow the transition to take place. Also, if the last ten projects crashed and burned, there may be some serious root problems that need to be corrected before launching the transition process. Finally, there may exist in a church many unresolved problems that could effectively squelch any effort to change. These, too, should be addressed before going forward.

Nevertheless, if you feel God is leading you in the direction of a New Testament cell-based ministry, then, yes, you should make the transition. If you are totally committed to equipping the saints to do the work of the ministry and to giving your ministry to the whole body, the answer is again yes; go ahead and do it! If the charter, bylaws, and governmental body of your church are flexible and serve the vision, yes; you should proceed.

Testimony of Bill and Sherry Gibson, Life Group Pastors at Embassy Christian Center, Laguna Hills, California (Roberts Liardon Ministries)

Since beginning to transition from a program-based church to a cell-based church, we have noticed that our people are more secure and connected to the church. Pastoral care within the cell group, as well as flowing from the cell groups, has contributed significantly to healthier church members.

The following components are some of the fundamental strengths we have discovered to be necessary to successfully transition a church to a cell-based ministry. With these strengths, our own transition at Bethany was made with a minimum of difficulty. If a church is lacking in one area or another, however, it should take the time to build those components into the ministry before transitioning. Remember also that God can supernaturally bring about change—and will—as we approach Him in faith and with earnest and humble hearts. He hears the cry and knows the desire of our hearts.

The Importance of a Strong Senior Pastor

There is no church board or committee that can inspire, lead, and bring about change as powerfully and effectively as can a strong senior pastor. In nearly every instance of successful and growing cell churches, God has a strong, visionary man at the helm leading the way.

Personally, I don't believe that implementation of the cell-church vision can be accomplished with a deacons' board or elders' board trying to lead the way. Successful transitioning requires a God-called leader who is able to marshal all other leaders and who is capable of rallying the troops. It is too easy, when the going gets rough, for a board to decide that it may not be such a good idea after all and cancel the cell-based ministry. Not even a strong "second-in-charge" can pull it off without the senior pastor's active involvement in the process. Only a strong senior pastor with influence and wisdom, one who is well established and full of vision, is capable of leading the charge into the long transition process that is required.

He inspires excellence.

The senior pastor needs to be able to inspire excellence in the cell-group leaders. To do so, he must be a man of excellent spirit himself. Mediocrity will slow any attempt at transitioning to a grinding halt. Therefore, the pastor must be an encourager and one that the majority is willing to follow into any endeavor. Anything less than excellence on the part of the leader will cause transitioning to be an uphill battle.

He has integrity.

A strong senior pastor must have integrity. Unless he exhibits this character trait, any project that he attempts has two strikes against it before it even begins. If the pastor does not demonstrate integrity, any gains made in cell-based ministry will be eventually lost as people begin to discern this flaw in his leadership. If he is not a man of character and principle, on what standards will he build the ministry? The congregation **must** have a sense that the person they are following in this radical shift of ministry is an honest and sincere person whom they can trust.

He is personally involved.

As explained in the preceding chapter of this book, cell-based ministry is not an addendum to existing ministry. Rather, it is the central focus and heart of everything that the church will do and try to accomplish. Not only must the pastor give vision and inspiration to the transition, but he must also be a vital part of the process. This is not a "y'all go ahead" ministry; it's a "follow me, let's do it together" ministry. The senior pastor, therefore, must lead the way by experiencing cell-group life for himself so that he can speak about it as one who knows it firsthand. When he can give testimonies from his own experience of the benefits of cell-group ministry, the congregation will gladly follow.

We have included another element of personal involvement by the senior pastor in the training and motivation of our cell leaders. In our monthly Leadership Summits, Pastor Larry meets with all the cell leadership as a group. He goes over the weekly facilitator guides and the vision for the month and then spends time encouraging and motivating the cell leaders to press on in their ministries. He ends the meeting with a time of prayer.

He has many credits, but few debits.

When implementing change and new concepts, nothing can take the place of a leader who has the trust and confidence of the church body. Because he has taken the people down many roads that have led to success and victory, they believe in him. His past actions add credit to his ministry and to his influence in the church. Where this respect and credibility are missing, it may be best to spend some time building credibility before a pastor starts such a critical transition. The same is true for new pastors, who would do well to cultivate patience and relationship before broadcasting new vision.

Team Management

Although the senior pastor is the key player, team involvement is also necessary in the cell church. A good example of the importance of teamwork is illustrated by an experiment conducted by NASA. This experiment formulated a test to teach astronauts the benefits of working as a team. The test established a scenario in which a spacecraft crashed on the moon, and the astronauts were required to find a solution to get back to the mother ship. Each person was tested separately; then the group was tested as a team. The results revealed that in nearly all cases, the team made decisions that were approximately 30% to 50% more accurate than the decisions made by individuals.

This same concept of team management is vital in implementing cell-group ministry. In the cell church, the senior pastor, the pastoral staff, and the individual cell groups compose the team. The team may be thought of as a "machine with human parts." Like any machine, each part is crucial to the next, and regular maintenance is required. There needs to be ongoing resolution of conflicts that cause "friction" and wear down other team members. Care must be taken to ensure that every part of the "machine" functions properly and gives needed input to the team.

Synergy

Weekly team meetings will help the ministry stay in the spirit of cell-based and cell-led ministry. These meetings should be for the purpose of engaging in open discussion, obtaining information, delegating of responsibilities, and brainstorming. This kind of weekly team meeting creates an atmosphere of ownership of the ministry among the leaders and allows each person to have a feel for what is going on. Slight adjustments that are necessary to answer the concerns of the constantly changing needs of the groups can be made at that time. These weekly meetings help to avoid major catastrophes that seem to come from nowhere after it's too late to do anything about them.

The cooperative spirit of these meetings creates what is known as synergy. Synergism is that cooperative effort which produces results greater than the sum of the results produced by the same leaders acting independently of one another. In the minds of the leadership, synergy sets in motion the type of cooperative effort needed in the cell groups for maximum achievement. What is often impossible to do with staff in the program-based church, because of its independent and divisive nature, is easily accomplished in the cell church with a cooperative and unified team concept.

Remember the instruction Paul gave to those at Ephesus. Ephesians 4:16 says, *"From whom the whole body fitly joined together and compacted by that which every joint supplieth, according to the effectual working in the measure of every part, maketh increase of the body unto the edifying of itself in love."* This is synergy!

The Makeup of a Successful Team

In order to successfully design and construct a building, you need people with differing gifts, management styles, and leadership abilities. No one person can effectively do all the work alone. The illustration of building a skyscraper will help you understand the dynamics involved in achieving a desired, finished product. The same principles apply to building a successful local cell-church ministry.

First of all, you need an **architect**. The architect is the visionary: he sees what needs to be built and possesses the creative gifts to communicate his vision on paper. He understands design and how it fits into the overall picture in the area in which he is working.

In the cell church, too, there must be a creative visionary giving clarity to the church and meaning to the cell concept. He must also be able to *communicate* the need and the practical benefits of the cell-church ministry to the individuals in the local body of believers.

Vision needs design. Alongside the visionary, the cell church needs those who can see the broader picture of possible obstacles, as well as the means for overcoming those obstacles. Such persons take the big idea and break it down to a step-by-step process that can be organized and accomplished by the next level of workers in the building process.

Thus, secondly, you need an **engineer**. The job of the engineer is to take the concept created by the architect and work on the feasibility and technical dynamics of the idea. He must refine the complicated aspects of the original idea and work out any conflicting data. The engineer also designs and devises strategy for every phase of the building process.

The third type of individual that you need in the building project is the **superintendent.** The superintendent has oversight of the entire building project. He is the agent of both the architect and the engineer who makes sure that the ideas and design are carried out through the entire construction process. He works with every level of the workers, supervising their work and making recommendations and corrections as the work is done.

He understands how the work is done and provides the necessary quality control over the work. The person in this position advances the idea to the practical, physical completion of the building.

Desperately needed in any cell-church ministry is this level of supervision. There will always be the need for someone to train and inspect the ministry on every level. When the cell ministry in the local church begins to falter, someone needs to be there to get feedback, observe, and make corrections. That person should also make sure that the results that the pastor wants are accomplished. To ensure that the vision is carried out to the finish, the superintendent works to bring the ministry to its satisfactory completion. Goals and results are accomplished by the work of the superintendent.

The fourth person needed in order to finish a building project is the **journeyman**. The journeyman is the *meister,* or skilled craftsman. He knows his trade well and understands exactly how to do his part. He takes the refined design, gets his tasks from the superintendent and, with other tradesmen, does the actual work of constructing the building. Alongside the journeyman is his helper, or **apprentice**. Having a helper to work beside him ensures the journeyman that future building projects will also be accomplished.

The cell church will go nowhere without highly trained individuals who know their work and how to perform it. Cell leaders who are skilled in what they do and understand the need to train others make cell-group ministry in the local church successful. Without this level of workers functioning and the leadership base growing, you will never build a successful ministry. You must give attention to building a highly skilled and motivated work force of leaders who can bring the energy and "know-how" to the daily tasks and functions of the cell church.

The Cell-Group Team

The cell group is a team that pulls together to perform all aspects of ministry tasks. Every function of the cell group is more effectively accomplished by team effort. The members of each group must see themselves as a team that works together as a caring community, a powerful prayer force, and as an evangelistic arm that reaches out to the friends and family members of each of the cell members.

A Strong Prayer Base

A Firm Foundation

Prayer provides the spiritual energy not inherent in our carnal nature. It is the foundation for launching the cell-group ministry, and it is the fuel that keeps it in orbit. Without prayer, we will lose our momentum and will come spiraling down to eventual failure. Prayer is the thrust behind cell-based ministry. It prepares the hearts of everyone involved to get ready for change by kindling vision; and then by promoting flexibility, it gives people the ability to cope with that change. When people pray, they expect God to do something new and different. Then, when cell-based ministry is introduced, they can embrace it as the new thing that God wants to do.

Intercession

Cell ministry around the world seems to find its strength through intensive prayer. In each of the cell churches that we visited, we discovered a strong intercessory prayer base. Ongoing intercessory prayer is directly related to the success of each cell group as well as to the effectiveness of the entire cell ministry. Such prayer gives God the opportunity to speak His purpose and will into the heart of each Christian.

Recently, one of our pastors surveyed every cell leader who was having success and multiplying his group. He also surveyed the unsuccessful leaders. The successful groups were fasting and holding prayer meetings; the failing groups were not. In Seoul, San Salvador, Singapore and anywhere else where there is successful cell ministry, we find dedication to intensive intercessory prayer. Without this kind of prayer, cell-group ministry cannot flourish, and, perhaps, cannot even survive.

Testimony of Pastor Carl Everett and wife Gaynell, Veteran Cell Leaders at Bethany World Prayer Center, Baker, Louisiana

As a husband-and-wife team, we have found that you have to have the power of God present with His Holy Spirit abiding. In the course of the seven years of cell ministry and being leaders, we have seen the effectiveness of fasting and praying. We cannot be effective without seeking God and denying the flesh.

On the day of the meeting we fast and pray; we also encourage members to do the same. As a team, we then join together and pray before the meeting. We come into agreement for the needs of those coming to the meeting and ask the presence of the Holy Spirit to abide to the uttermost in our hearts. When this happens, we are open to what the Lord wants to do in the meeting. We cleanse our own hearts and keep them pure, even in our own relationship to each other. We don't give ground to the enemy's devices with any grievances towards one another—instead, maintaining forgiveness and favor with one another.

As we have done this through the years, we have seen so many miracles. One lady came in with a walking cane, needing a hip replacement. As we prayed for her that night, the power of God touched her and healed her. She went out the door swinging the cane and walking without a limp.

God's anointing and blessing is present as we seek Him on behalf of the calling He has brought us into: our members.

Values Transformation

Every church and many pastors are looking for some program that will take the work out of Christianity. Cell-group ministry is not the answer to that problem! In fact, cell groups probably require more work than anyone in your congregation has ever been asked to do for God. Nevertheless, there is much fruit that results from cell ministry and that will bring a sense of satisfaction and fulfillment to people like nothing else they have ever been involved in.

If effective cell ministry is to be accomplished, however, there must first be a transformation of the values system in our lives. I Corinthians 16:15 says, *"I beseech you, brethren, (ye know the house of Stephanas, that it is the firstfruits of Achaia, and [that] they have **addicted** themselves to the ministry of the saints)."* We need a sense that we have been bought by Jesus Christ, that we are His and not our own. Only such awareness will enable us to make the sacrifices necessary to fulfill this new ministry. The internalizing of these values takes time—sometimes even years—to happen on a church-wide basis. You can see how prayer accelerates the adoption of such values as we open our hearts to move onto God's time-table.

No Time

During a cell-group seminar in a major U. S. city, a pastor told me, "Brother Billy, I just don't see how cell ministry can work in our major metropolitan city. With Little League, soccer teams, and football games going on, our families' schedules are absorbed. They have no time for any other meetings." This is the value system that has permeated many churches today, resulting in families that have no control over their own time. Help your congregation prioritize according to the biblical value system of commitment and sacrifice. Remember that it will take time for these values to be internalized.

A Hunger and Thirst for Ministry

God has given us a promise that the spiritually hungry and thirsty will be satisfied. As dynamic cell ministry touches the lives of people in your congregation, they will begin to aspire to leadership. As they grow and are equipped, they will model this new style of leadership before others in your church. As the others see the new Christian taking his place in vibrant ministry in the cell group, they too will acquire a thirst and a hunger for this ministry. As more of the church members experience New Testament ministry as it was intended to be, things that compete with it will begin to lose their appeal. There is a quenching flood of fulfillment and satisfaction for all who desire to participate in this effective ministry.

Evangelism Mentality

Maintaining a vision for reaching the lost is a challenge that must be met. Danny Ost, a great missionary to Mexico, stated, "We must look at the lost through Jesus' contact lenses." If we really understand the condition of the lost soul, how can we not do something about it? Evangelism should begin with people with whom you already have relationships. Start there, and then branch out to others who cross your path. (See also Chapter 10, "Reaching Your Personal Community.") In his book, *Your Church Has a Fantastic Future*, Dr. Robert Schuller states, *"Find a need and meet it; find a hurt and heal it."*[1] This is the spirit of the cell church. For effective ongoing evangelism strategies to survive, you must adopt the following philosophy. "Feed the sheep, focus on the lost." Every pastor is required to provide weekly biblical instruction to his congregation, but must also moti-

---

[1] From the inside cover quote on "The Secret to Success"

vate his congregation to reach out to the lost and hurting people in their community.

Evangelism through the Cells

Let the cell groups themselves be the platform for reaching the lost through friendship evangelism. Then, occasionally plan major evangelistic events that are designed to *feed the cells.* But this can be accomplished only if the cell groups are directly involved in the effort and only if the cell groups participate in intensive follow-up on all the converts resulting from such events. The effectiveness of relationship evangelism, however, far exceeds the effectiveness of event evangelism. Close to eighty percent of all Christians in church attendance today are there because they knew someone who had a relationship with Christ and shared it with them.

Rotating into Every Field

When visiting a church in Indiana, I stayed in a home that was situated in the middle of several large cornfields. As I watched the fields being harvested, I realized that no matter how full the field had been before the harvesting began, afterwards, there was little left but gleanings. The same is true in cell ministry. After a meeting has been held a couple of times in one host home, it is beneficial to rotate to the homes of other cell-group members. This allows every member to have the opportunity to invite relatives, friends, and neighbors to the meeting at his own home.

Many of our relatives and friends are reluctant to go to a stranger's home but would be open to coming to the home of someone with whom they have an established relationship. Consequently, part of our strategy includes rotating into the home of each cell member for two weeks, then moving to the next home. By following this method, every field that is ripe unto harvest can be reaped.

Strong Family Values

The most fertile soil for evangelism is within a believer's family. That fact proved true in my own family. After my conversion, many of my family members also came to Christ, including one of my brothers who is now a pastor in a nearby city. I counted the number of family members that came to Christ since I became Christian. This included the in-laws of my brothers and sisters as well as my own in-laws. The number has risen to over forty members that have come to Christ since my conversion.

Building strong moral values in families sets them up for conversion later in life. When a family already has strong moral values, it is much more easily influenced by the Gospel of Christ.

Reclaiming the Home

Many families today have lost their spiritual emphases in their homes. When more attention is given to Roseanne than to Romans, and to Nintendo rather than to Nehemiah, families lose vital spiritual life. But the local church that teaches and trains its membership to have strong family values will find that cell ministry is the most natural step in ministry to the home. Families that begin having cell-group meetings in their homes can recapture their spiritual emphases. In homes where believers meet to pray and care for one another, there is a refocusing on Christ.

A good example of this refocusing occurred in the life of one of the teenagers in our church. Chris, the son of a former administrator of the church, had a typical teenager's bedroom, decorated with the posters of basketball stars. However, after becoming involved in cell groups with his family and with the teen ministry in our church, those posters came down, and a map of China went up, along with Scripture verses that guided his life. At this writing, Chris is preparing for a life of missions ministry in China.

Discipleship and Training

Jesus, the Apostle Paul, and many other great Bible patriarchs spent their lifetimes mentoring and discipling potential leaders. Time spent in training and in one-on-one discipleship is invaluable to the success of cell-group ministry. Without it there will always be a shortage of leadership. We need, therefore, to cultivate a mentality and to develop a strategy that lends itself to constant awareness of raising up an expanding leadership base. A plan for locating and training new leaders must be implemented for continued growth and expansion.

Testimony of Pastor Don Lyon, Rockford, Illinois

Our church was strongly program-based, therefore the transition process was much more difficult for us than it is for some. Today, we are thrilled with every cell group we have and what God has done in developing leadership through cells. To think that at one time the leadership base was a very small group at the head of this organization, but now there is a very broad base of leadership all through the congregation.

We have testimonies on a regular basis of people being healed, delivered, families brought together, and every other kind of victory accomplished. To read these testimonies is like reading the book of Acts all over again!

Training

There is a great return on any investment made in the lives of people. People should always be our focus, as success begins and ends with people. Training in doctrine, in counseling skills, and in practical ministry and management is fundamental to the accomplishment of the cell-ministry vision. The expanding numbers of cell leaders are the "front line" servants and soldiers of the church, and they need to be fully equipped and prepared for all that the staff is asking of them. Remember also that leadership requires sacrifice. At various times, our cell leaders, "twelve" leaders, and pastors have all had to give up the Wednesday night preaching/ teaching services in order to receive training and focus. This is the price of being a leader and carrying out the vision of the house.

Biblically Based, Holy Spirit Led

Nothing can take the place of a strong emphasis on the Scripture-based evidence of cell ministry, and that knowledge will impart spiritual strength to cell-group members. In each cell meeting, the group should give a sincere invitation to the Holy Spirit to lead and guide them as ministry takes place.

Bible-Based

Anything that is not Bible based and "Holy Spirit led" will have to be maintained in the flesh. Cell-group ministry is too spiritual in nature to be sustained by the efforts of man. Once the paradigm shift has been made, the strong Bible-based church will be able to see the validity of cell ministry as proven in the Bible. When the Christian can look in the Bible and say, "It's in there," he will be convinced by the Word and will "get on board." Until the mental shift has been made, however, the present filter used for viewing blocks out the Word as it pertains to house-to-house ministry.

Holy Spirit Led

Openness to the moving of the Holy Spirit in the cell groups is essential to real New Testament ministry. Unless the Holy Spirit is allowed to freely move within the structure of cell groups, we have nothing more than a structure. Thus, during the cell-group meeting, the Holy Spirit should be given the liberty to convict, heal, empower, and baptize believers. Spiritual gifts should flow as part of every meeting. Powerful deliverance and healing can be experienced when the Holy Spirit is allowed to have His way at a cell meeting. Let Him touch lives. Whatever we do, we want to obey the instruction found in I Thessalonians 5:19, *"Quench not the Spirit."*

Accountability

Accountability to leadership and local church authority is indispensable in the cell-church concept. Avoid any appearance of the "loose cannon" type of ministry in which the leader answers to no one. This is an invitation for the enemy to seek out weak members of the group to bring division and to destroy relationships. We cannot guarantee that division will never happen, but accountability lessens the probability of its occurrence.

High Touch

Cell ministry must include an emphasis on visitation. When cell members are visited by the leadership and other cell-group members, an opportunity arises for ministry to occur. Dr. Yonggi Cho said, *"Ministry visitation is essential. When a person belongs to our congregation, he should be regularly visited by pastors and lay-leaders."* [2] Also, people always seem to do better when they know that someone is watching and showing concern for them.

---

[2] As quoted by Dr. Karen Hurston, *Building the World's Largest Church*, Gospel Publishing House, 1994, p. 114.

A "paper trail" of weekly attendance and activity reports should also be in place so that the cell-group leader records who is in attendance and what happened in the cell meeting. He should then pass on this information to the pastoral staff to examine. Such reports can keep the pastors informed of the needs in the cell groups, thus becoming a tool for the church to know best how to serve and minister to the people. Proper accountability for all will be fostered in this way.

Correct Cell Structure

When everything else is "right," the proper cell-group structure and format will serve to ensure success. What works for us, as far as structure and format are concerned, may need to be altered to suit your situation. Find what works for you and stick with it. If everything else is right but you fail on cell-group night, you will lose impetus and energy. People will stop coming to an ailing cell group.

Remember that you are moving into an entirely new way of ministry. Don't expect that following the recommendations of the latest manual on the subject will be enough to implement this ministry. You will need all the ability that you have and all that God can give to successfully make the transition to a cell church. When you do, however, the transition will bring you into an exciting and dynamic New Testament ministry.

Chapter 6

How to Transition into a Cell-Group Church

A high school coach was attempting to motivate his players to persevere through a difficult schedule. Halfway through, he stood before his team and asked, "Did Michael Jordan ever quit?"

The team shouted "No!"

"Did Larry Bird ever quit?"

The team resounded "No!"

"Did Magic Johnson ever quit?"

Again the team screamed "No!"

"Did Elmer McAllister ever quit?"

There was a long silence. Finally one player was bold enough to ask, "Who was Elmer McAllister? We never heard of him."

The coach snapped back, "Of course you never heard of him—he quit!" [1]

Transition is like a long basketball season with many opponents. You must face each one with determination and focus. Decide now that you will see it through to the end. "Don't Quit!"

Understand What Stays and What Goes

When a local church has spent the last twenty years developing programs that have become the foundation of its ministry, it is often difficult, though not impossible, to transition into the cell-church model. To transition is "to pass from one form or stage to another." In transitioning to a cell church, your goal is not to destroy years of hard work or to invalidate the good that you have done, but is simply to improve the quality of ministry at your church and to make it more efficient. Therefore, slowly prepare your church for change without dropping all programs in one fell swoop. To do so would be too much of a shock to the congregation, the leaders, and the volunteers and would leave them feeling abandoned. Thus, take your time, and carefully consider the value that each program has for the church and

---

[1] *Good Stuff*, Progressive Business Publications, Malvern, PA, February 2000

those involved before eliminating it. There is no need to stop everything overnight; use wisdom in the transition process.

The ministries that need to be maintained are those that support a successful Sunday worship service. (Since beginning the cell ministry, we call our Sunday morning worship service a celebration service.) Therefore, avoid doing anything that would compromise the success of the worship service. Cell-group ministry should bring more life and meaning to the celebration service; consequently, be careful not to neglect the celebration service for the sake of cell groups.

There are always two considerations regarding decisions in the transition process: celebration and cells. What happens in the celebration services should support cell-group ministry, and what happens in the cell groups should support the celebration services. **The cells should reinforce what is said in the pulpit, and the pulpit should reinforce what is done in the cells.** The New Testament Church met not just house to house but also in the temple. As Acts 5:42 says, *"And daily in the temple, and in every house, they ceased not to teach and preach Jesus Christ."* It is important to be aware of the benefits of both types of ministry. Although these are two different ministries, they should be able to interface. Focus on cells, but don't overlook the powerful results of the large congregational meeting.

There are specific logistical concerns that require special staff during celebration services. Ushers, nursery workers, parking lot attendants, choir members and other essential ministries will always be necessary and, thus, should be maintained. Such ministry situations are peculiar to the celebration service. Though these are not directly related to cells, they do not compete or interfere with cells. The staff members involved in these areas should be members of weekly cell groups. Parking lot attendants, ushers, and greeters may also have a staff person over them who should be involved in cells. Members from cell groups may rotate quarterly to embellish these weekly and ongoing helps ministries.

Don't Lose Your Identity

It is important to maintain your identity in the community in which you have been working over the years. Avoid the temptation to "trash" everything that you have been doing and to start all over with a different image.

By following the transition steps in the next few paragraphs, you will be able to prepare your congregation and community for the fact that you are becoming a cell church. Remember that you want to increase your effectiveness through cell ministry without destroying established identity. When a movement requires you to lose your identity, most times that movement is a cult. The cell-based church should increase your effectiveness and the efficiency of your ministry.

At Bethany we have been able to maintain our vision for prayer, world missions, and other vital ministries that identify us as Bethany World Prayer Center to the community. As we transitioned to a cell church, we kept the values that made us successful while learning others that made us more "New Testament." Decide now that as you transition into a cell-based ministry, you will maintain and improve the unique strengths of ministry that God has given you. You will still be the same church, with the same identity; only now you will be more effective in everything you do.

Steps to Take

As you begin transitioning, each of your programs will need to be assimilated into the cell ministry. I can tell you right now that some programs will take longer than others. For example, the Christian education department will take much longer to assimilate into the cell context than will the follow-up team or the choir. Determine each program's "life expectancy." Set a course for its termination, then begin to take it off "life support."

What constitutes life support for programs? Staff, lay leaders, volunteers, budget dollars, and promotion by the pastor from the pulpit. Start the termination process by first stopping the promotion, then the budget, and then redirect the staff, leaders, and volunteers toward cell-group ministry. As other members ask to become involved in these programs, just let them know that the church is moving into cell ministry and that the programs are being assimilated into cell-based ministry. Then invite them to participate in the cell ministry.

Favorite Programs

During assimilation of programs into cell ministry, there can be no **"golden calves"** left in the stall. Every pet program that remains must be assimilated into cell groups or terminated if not sufficiently related to cell ministry. If any *favorite programs* are preserved, they will become the door back to the old paradigm when the cell ministry starts encountering obstacles that are normal in the transition process. Every program can be assimilated in time. Don't spare one and assimilate the others. Use wisdom and take courage to place all the ministry possible at the cell-group level.

Make sure that the cell leaders and members are ready to assume the **ministry function** of the old program before terminating that program. For example, before letting the cell group take over follow-up, make sure that the leaders are *trained* in follow-up. The same holds true for hospital visitation, counseling, and other ministries.

As you transition, you want to be sure not to lose the benefits that the programs provided. Your goal is to *increase* benefits and efficiency in the transition to the cell-church model.

Transition Model

Much of what we have talked about so far deals with understanding the philosophy and biblical foundations of the cell-group church. Although a good understanding of the cell concept is paramount in making a successful transition, the transition itself is a very important step in bringing the entire church into the cell-group structure. The following discussion describes a model that will apply to most churches preparing to make that transition.

Research

Research every aspect of the cell-church structure by reading as many books as possible on the subject. This will expose you to many different perspectives on how cell groups work. There are many models from which to choose. You may need to borrow from several to come up with the model best suited to your local situation. Since the Holy Spirit is not confined to any one model, discover what He is doing in several churches that are involved in cell groups. He may even give you something unique for your church!

It is even more important to **go see for yourself** how different models work. On-site inspection is more valuable in gaining understanding of the cell-church model than just reading books on the subject. You will "catch" the vision and the understanding that you need as you observe the people of the cell church in action. How they serve, how they communicate, the vision of each one, and the excitement of the ministry are all important images to which you need to be exposed in order to fully appreciate the dynamics of the cell church. Many of our pastors, including Pastor Larry, visited the great cell churches in San Salvador, Singapore, Seoul, and, eventually, in Bogotá. Each time we visited a cell church, we came back with greater understanding and vision.

Testimony of Pastor Jake Benton, Bethany World Prayer Center, Baker, Louisiana (Pastor Benton has been on staff at Bethany since before the transition to cells, and he went on the first trip of staff pastors down to El Salvador in 1993).

My first impression of the cell structure in the church in El Salvador was that it was impacting the entire nation. What was occurring at Elim was not being done in a corner or in isolation, they talked and lived and breathed it.

I saw that the model worked, and not just for a few, but that it was contagious and affecting the entire church. The church was not doing a lot of things; they all were focused on cells. They filled the church. They arrived in buses that were packed full of people excited about coming to church. That showed me they were hungry for God and for souls and that church was satisfying their appetite.

*In my mind's eye I still can see multitude of people; they were like a tidal wave coming in and out of their district cell offices. They were so eager to serve the church that they had to schedule each zone so that they took turns and didn't have **too many** sign up for a particular day. I was amazed at their spirit, mind and willingness to serve without prompting and figured that if it worked in El Salvador it could work at Bethany, too.*

Informing Others: The Pastor's Job

Take the time necessary to condition your leaders and congregation to this new direction. Most people have difficulty with change, no matter how beneficial it may be to them. Once you are convinced of the general direction in which you want to go, begin to communicate to your leaders how God is leading you, and help them "share in the vision." *Do not surprise everyone on Sunday morning by announcing, "Starting today, we are now a cell church!"* Such a major shift in ministry direction should not come as a surprise to your congregation. If it does, they may have some surprises for you!

Inform your leaders in detail about the new direction that the church is about to take, and give them time to gain appreciation for it. Send them to successful cell churches to see the benefits of cell ministry, and answer their questions. After you have gained their support, begin to share the idea in "bits and pieces" with the congregation. It is not necessary to drop a bombshell on the church immediately after the elders agree to head in this new direction, but rather teach the people and give them time to adjust to this new way of thinking. We started our own transition by simply announcing to our Gideon's Army intercessors that we were starting prayer cells and that we would begin a time of training on Saturdays. They came and soon were involved in the first groups that we had. Someone said, *"If people are equally informed, they seldom disagree."* I add to that, *"If people don't agree, give them more information."*

Transition takes time. Most churches take three to five years to complete the transition process. You can't rush into the cell-church model like you do some new Sunday School program. A major change in the value system of your ministry and congregation is necessary before the cell-church concept can be fully implemented. In his book, *The Second Reformation*, Bill Beckham talks about the ICC syndrome, **instant cell church syndrome**. This syndrome addresses the idea that we often want to change structure and have immediate success without having to change values. However, to have a functional and successful cell church, we must first define and internalize the New Testament values of such a church.

Prayer Training

Build the base for cell ministry upon prayer. Take ten or twelve weeks to train your congregation on intercessory prayer by holding classes or showing videos on the subject. As I have mentioned earlier, we used the Suzette Hattingh video series[2] with great success. After the prayer training is finished, you will know who are the most faithful members in the

---

[2] *Intercession as a Lifestyle Video Series,* Distributed by: Marilyn Neubauer, P. O. Box 302, Vista, California 92085. (760) 730-1808.

church: These people will compose your original cell groups.

Prayer is the single most important facet of the successful cell-church model. Once you realize that prayer is the launching pad and the unseen power that keeps the cell-church ministry in orbit, you will want to constantly remind, retrain, and refocus your church on prayer.

Cell-Group Training

After the original prayer cells and their leaders are chosen, begin a twelve-week training session for the leaders. Use this book or other books to build your training lessons. This training should coincide with the forming of the first groups. The people in our prayer cells received ten weeks of training on cell-group ministry before we actually launched our groups. They remained in the ongoing training for the next two years as we developed the cell ministry.

Testimony of Dr. Carroll Parish, Louisville, Kentucky

We began last year with six prototype cells, one of which multiplied 3 months later. Two months after that we had our church-wide kickoff of the cell ministry. We started with 26 cells in this congregation of 400, that is 76% of the membership in cells.

In preparing the Board, staff and cell leaders, we used your Christianity 101, Discipleship 201 and Leadership 301 training materials, as well as some other cell materials. So far we have had 2 salvations and 3 marriages saved that were on the verge of divorce.

Leadership Cells—Building Your "Twelve"

Start with Leadership Cells

Choose the leaders whom you want to mentor to form the original "circle of twelve." Beginning with a leadership group will provide an atmosphere in which you can make mistakes, ask questions, and create a workable format before exposing the entire church to cells. It is important to work out the "bugs" before you open the groups up to the church. Every member of this original leadership group will begin the leadership training process. By the end of the training process, everyone involved in the leadership group will have the necessary experience and confidence to lead his or her own group. During this training time, these leaders should be locating people whom they want to include in their own circle-of-twelve meeting.

Each week, the leader of the twelve should review one of the lessons from the leadership base path in order to gain more understanding of the concepts that are being implemented. This will equip each leader to train others in discipleship and leadership skills. After the twelve weeks, you should be able to multiply the group. Since the original twelve are leaders, they will be able to start groups of their own. Observe on the next page how multiplication occurs from the principle of twelve.

Multiply the Leadership Cells

As multiplication occurs, you should have new groups with at least four members each. At this time, each group member will go to friends and others in the congregation who they want to attend their new group and personally invite them. During this period you will start implementing all aspects of cell-group ministry. Mentor/protégé relationships should begin to form, bringing new people into each circle of twelve. The leader will be responsible for ensuring that each of his "twelve" goes through all the training classes and other training events. The mentor will take the new member through a class such as *Christianity 101* and on an *Encounter Weekend.* This portion of the discipleship process takes about six weeks. Then the new believer goes through discipleship and leadership training, follow-up, visitation, and prayer. In short, every other aspect of cell-group life should begin to be implemented. Groups should be able to grow to twelve members each from friends, new converts, and other church members. Each should then multiply by opening new groups.

During the first six-month period, you should start preparing the congregation to get involved with cell groups. Many will have already gotten involved, but teaching from the pulpit will reinforce what is taking place in the cell groups.

Open to Congregation

With several groups operating, you should be able to accommodate

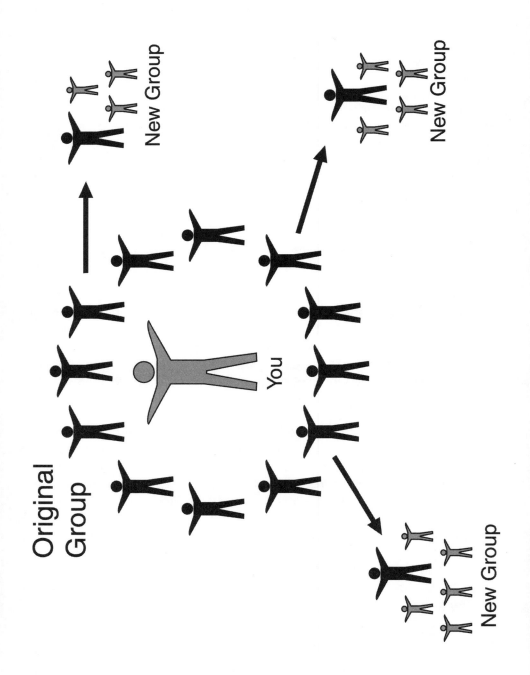

others in the congregation who are ready to become involved in cell groups. By this time your leaders will have had several months of experience with the cell groups and should be able to present cell ministry to the church in an effective and exciting way.

One way that we invited the congregation to get involved in cell groups was by passing out and collecting "I am interested in cell groups" cards on special "cell-group emphasis weeks." By using this technique, the cell-group members were able to follow up on each person from the information on the card. This has been an effective tool in finding those who have an interest in cells but are not sure how to get involved.

Through personal invitation by cell-group members and through encouragement from the pulpit, the cell ministry will begin to take center stage. As the interest level in the congregation increases, the number of cell groups in the church should also begin to grow steadily.

Create Homogeneous Groups

Just as the human body is composed of many different parts with separate needs and functions, so the community in which you live is also multi-faceted. In his book *House to House*[3], Larry Kreider explains that there are "groups" in each community that are in a specific location and have special needs, just as organs in the human body are located in specific places and have special needs and functions.

Family groups, which are located in subdivisions throughout the community, are comparable to the skin that covers the whole body. They are the most common and the most noticeable of the groups. However, there are also natural groups of people that come together on a daily or weekly basis to which our family groups do not appeal. These groups are often, but not always, workplace groups. Like organs in the human body, they, too, are located in a specific place, have a specific need, and perform a specific function. These groups of people are identified by the place where they meet, the need that they possess, or the function that they perform in the community. Such groups might be composed of fellow employees, single parents, police officers, homemakers, or any other group of people with a common interest. The possibilities are literally endless, limited only

---

[3] Published by House to House Publications, Ephrata, PA.

by your own creativity. You can identify any of these groups, however, by the shared criteria of place, need, or function.

For example, it may be difficult to persuade a medical doctor to come to your home for a meeting, but he may be open to meeting with his nursing staff and hospital administrator while making his rounds in the hospital. The same could be true for plant workers, shift workers, and other people who share similarities in occupation, recreation, or need.

Staff Considerations

It is necessary not to get too "top-heavy" with staff when you first start the cell-group ministry. You may already have several full-time staff members who are department heads, plus their assistants. Start with as few district pastor leaders as possible. For example, at Bethany we had ten full-time pastors on staff when we began the transition. We began by making two of these pastors district pastors, and the rest became zone pastors. As the number of cell groups grew, we increased the necessary number of district pastors and brought new zone pastors on staff. You should allow all the pastors, regardless of title, to act as cell leaders to start with in order to learn every phase of cell-group ministry. (This will become a natural occurrence with the principle-of-twelve model.)

Single staff churches, where the pastor is the only one on staff, need not rush into hiring staff. Wait until it is absolutely necessary before bringing on new staff. You will know it is time for new staff when the administration of the cell groups is taking all of your time, or when you have so many groups that you can't keep up with the new leaders. It is always necessary to be able to maintain strong relationships with leaders in the cell church. Be selective, as wrong leaders will cause problems as the church grows.

Commitment to Staffing Properly

Normal church structure requires a pastor to serve as a department head over a program or particular ministry. The youth department has a youth pastor; the evangelism department, an evangelism pastor; the missions department, a missions pastor; etc. In the same manner, churches with small groups often have a small-groups pastor. With the cell church, however, all pastoral positions exist for the purpose of cell groups. There are no other ministry positions in which to place pastors.

In the program-based church, the tendency is to put one pastor over all the cell groups and then expect him to take care of all the growth and training concerning cells. Unless you eventually increase the number of staff pastors working with him, that pastor will become overloaded, and the cell-group ministry will begin to flounder. As you add more cell groups, you must also commit to adding pastoral staff. Pastors are essential to facilitating the dynamics of growth and pastoral relationships through their interaction with cell leaders and cell members. They are key under-shepherds who are under the direction of the senior pastor.

In our own experience at Bethany, we first committed to add zone pastors as the number of cell groups grew at a 25/1 ratio. We have since discovered that with the principle of twelve, that ratio can be as much as one pastor for 50 cell groups, or even more. You will know when it is necessary to add pastoral staff by the workload on the existing staff. The Senior Pastor should develop his "Twelve" and only add staff as he needs to.

Never give up! As your cell church matures, you will begin to see an increasing leadership base and growth in all areas of ministry in your church. There can be those months, however, in which it seems that the ministry has stagnated. Those are times in which your perseverance is critical. Your commitment to equipping the believers, providing pastoral care, and empowering the members of the congregation will help you through those struggling times. I have talked to many pastors who have gone through difficult times but persevered and eventually became successful. They realized that there was really nothing any better or more fruitful than the cell structure to which to return. But with the passage of time, steadfastness of heart, and reliance on the Lord, success will come!

Read and think about this bit of wisdom shared by Calvin Coolidge.

Nothing in the world will take the place of persistence. Talent will not; nothing is more common than the unsuccessful person with talent. Genius will not; unrewarded genius is almost a proverb. Education will not; the world is full of educated derelicts. Persistence and determination alone are omnipotent. The slogan "press on" has solved and always will solve the problems of the human race.

Chapter 7

Casting Vision, Setting Goals, and Solving Problems

What would you do if you were not afraid?

Ever think of what you would do if you were the President of the United States, or a multi-billionaire? We often dream of lands we would visit, great deeds we would do, or ministries that we would build to reach millions of people. Well... why don't we do it? Are the goals that you set for yourself done in moments of "stark reality," or in your dreams? Who would you approach for a multi-million dollar loan for a new building, or for the opportunity to share something with them that could change their life, their future, their country?

Now is the time to get vision from God for the great things that He has in mind for you to accomplish. Now is the time for you to plan on being great for God, allowing Him to use you to fulfill all things that you dreamed of doing for His glory. Now is the time.

Dream Big

Someone has said, "Dream no small dreams, for they have no power to move the hearts of men." True to this statement, almost every pastor with whom I talk has a God-given vision burning in his soul for his city or particular area of ministry. He yearns to accomplish the great things that God wants to do through him and his church. However, before that vision can be realized, there must often be years of preparation, hard work, and conquering of mountains that block the way. In my opinion, cell-based ministry is the only way to fulfill the vision to reach our diverse, rapidly changing cities. Even in the cell church, however, there will be major problems to solve. This chapter prepares leaders for the challenge of keeping the cell vision alive and for solving problems that may arise in the implementation of the vision.

Loss of Vision

One of the fastest ways to fail at any endeavor is to lose the vision. It is

important, therefore, to keep the vision before the entire cell group structure at all
times. Every level of ministry should communicate vision—from the pulpit to the
home cell group. The church in El Salvador refers to this unity of vision as "Super-
Vision." When we communicate SUPER-
VISION to each person in the cell church,
we solve many motivational problems. But
if the vision is lost along the way, people
will start asking, "Why are we doing this?"
They need to know why they are doing
what they are doing and then be consumed
with that vision. The more "Super-Vision"
we give them, the less supervision they
need.

"Contra-Vision" is a term I coined to define any activity or talk that speaks
against the vision of the house. We must have the vision so clearly defined that we can recognize any departure from it. To avoid "Contra-Vision," the vision must be constantly rehearsed in everyone's heart and
mind. If a leader begins to speak against the need for multiplication or
evangelism, for example, "Contra-Vision" begins to take its toll on the group.
But if you keep the vision for evangelism, growth, and multiplication alive,
you can overcome "Contra-Vision."

In carrying out any vision, many mundane tasks and routine prepara-
tions must be performed. Filling out weekly reports, attending training and
briefing sessions, and phoning cell members are only a few examples of
such tasks. Without "Super-Vision," the leadership will fall behind in these
rudimentary tasks, and the productivity of the group will wane. Keeping the
vision fresh, however, fuels excitement, even when leaders are carrying
out menial tasks.

Four Stages in Implementing the Vision

- **Communicate the vision** — Vision comes from the architect, who,
  generally, is the pastor. Someone has to have the vision for the cell-
  church model and be able to effectively communicate that vision to the
  leadership of the local church. When you "say it," enough people will

rise out of their pews and join in to make the endeavor a success. If the vision is not effectively communicated, however, it may never become a reality.

The accomplishment of the vision that God has given our church for the Baton Rouge area will require years of labor by hundreds of people. These many people must work tirelessly, full of the vision that God has given our church. Without vision, there is no fuel for the soul. Without fuel for the soul, we become apathetic and lazy; and in this late hour of the Church, there is no time for apathy or laziness.

Vision alone is like faith without works. It cannot, in itself, produce practical results that are measurable and tangible. If having a vision were all that was necessary, ministry would be easy. However, vision must have "legs" to carry out the works. Those legs come in the form of focus, action, and problem solving. The architect who envisions great buildings or complex structures must be able to communicate his ideas with such clarity that those who are responsible for the actual construction can also grasp the vision. I have seen cathedrals in Europe whose designs would have been totally beyond my ability to conceive without first seeing the plans. Like the builders, I could understand the architect's vision only by first viewing his plans. Then and only then could the workers carry out the task of constructing such an extraordinary structure. Vision, too, must be broken into its simplest components; action must also be taken on each component of that vision if it is to come to pass.

The vision that God has given us at Bethany is to plant one thousand cell groups in the Baton Rouge area. Our goal is to have healthy cell groups located in every neighborhood of our city, reaching out to the needs of that neighborhood and evangelizing every person in that area. Each of these groups will have well-trained leaders who can provide pastoral care for each person in the group.

This great vision is so well communicated from the pulpit and in the cell groups that it produces a fire in the soul of the church, building expectancy for great accomplishments. The communication of the vision also challenges us to be successful in carrying the vision to its conclusion. Sometimes vision is so great it seems almost impossible to accomplish. When vision is communicated and then not carried out, credibility can be compromised. Bob Biehl, president of Masterplanning Group,

International, states, "If visibility exceeds your ability, it will destroy your credibility."[1] As one of the implementers of the vision at Bethany, along with our entire pastoral staff, I often pray that God will give us the ability to carry out the vision of building one thousand cell groups in the Baton Rouge area. Without this ability, we will not be able to achieve the vision of the church.

- **Establish goals** — Did you catch that comment that prayer is needed? Please keep in mind that prayer is always the first step, and it is part of every other step. Nowhere is it more essential to have God's clear direction than in the phase of setting goals. Having goals for growth is vital. Without goals, how will we be able to measure success? The establishment of goals should include several different dimensions.

There should be a numerical goal. This numerical goal should be based on the demographics of the area in which you are ministering. Be realistic, yet dare to stretch your faith in setting the numerical goals God is placing in your heart.

There should be a time goal, that is, how long it will take to accomplish the goal. The time goal should be broken down into a five-year or long-term goal, a one-year goal, and a ninety-day goal. The ninety-day goal is easily monitored on a monthly basis, whereas a five-year goal is difficult to monitor based on a one-month period of activity.

There must be a marketing goal, or a method, by which to get the message out to all interested parties. This may not sound spiritual to you, but it is very important. When I was a missionary in Germany in the late '80s, my mission office produced a very informative, full-color, thirty-two page Christian magazine that targeted all of the German-speaking nations. At several conferences, it was hailed by the conference organizers as one of the best magazines in Germany. Many even considered it the best Christian magazine available in the German language. We spent untold hours working on the content, graphics, layout and design of that magazine. The only problem with the magazine was that we had no plan for marketing it to the German-speaking nations for which it was designed. Consequently, after a year had passed and four issues had been published, we did not have enough sales to justify the continuation

---

[1] Bob Biehl, *Stop Setting Goals*, Ballantine Books, 1995, p. 119.

of the magazine.

It is just as important in the cell church to have a method by which the goals of the cell church are kept in front of the people in a positive way. We did this by producing videos to show the benefits of cell groups to the congregation, by performing skits for Sunday services, and by distributing printed material to keep the concept forever in front of their eyes. This has been our marketing plan.

There must be an ongoing process of problem solving. If you are not reaching your numerical goals, solve the problem. If you are not reaching your time goals or marketing goals, find out why and correct the problem. Until the problems that prevent you from reaching your goals are solved, you will never attain success.

Problem solving is an everyday, weekly, and ongoing process. *Never let a problem go unresolved for more than ninety days.* Many times, we may notice a minor problem but put off dealing with it for a while. By immediate attention to and resolution of the problem, however, we can discover reasons for failing to reach other goals. Don't delay dealing with obvious problems because one problem may be covering up several others.

Churches around the nation are looking for a pure cell-church model in the United States that can be reproduced in their cities. In the process of becoming a cell church, you will encounter many problems, such as a shortage of leaders, inexperience in cell ministry, and difficulty in changing from the old paradigm of the program-based church. But as you overcome the numerous obstacles to cell-church ministry, you will gain the confidence to carry out the vision. The more problems you solve, the more confidence you have. Confidence grows not only as you see results from the structure that you have, but also as you effectively solve new problems that arise.

- **Extend the challenge** — In Chapter 9, "The Mature Cell-Church Model," I discuss building a predictable system that follows a clear set of goals for what you want your cell-church model to be like when it becomes mature. Goals for developing leadership, motivation, community, and personal ministry by everyone in the cell groups need to be clearly defined. For example, if the groups are having problems bonding, what will you do to promote stronger, closer relationships? Once goals are defined, you must start solving problems that impede the obtaining of those goals. Goals should not be numerical only, but should also be quality oriented. You should have quarterly goals for solving prevailing problems, goals for improving working conditions for staff and cell leadership, goals for motivation, goals for improving community in the cell-group structure, and, of course, numerical goals. You will find that as you solve problems that prevent growth, you will automatically grow to a certain degree, whether you have numerical goals or not. But the motivation required to reach goals must sometimes come from something not as obvious and planned. That's where challenge comes in.

Challenge is requiring someone to achieve through the exercise of boldness. In the great vision of the local church, amidst all its goal setting and promotion, there must come a challenge that provokes boldness in each of us to take on the task against all odds. Understanding that we are taking back all that the enemy has stolen from us, for God's glory, is the challenge. Without challenge, the work can become "ho-hum." Don't ever forget that Jesus Christ is working with us to accomplish great things for Him.

- **Develop a plan** — The plan arises out of vision and Spirit-led direction. That brings us back to time spent in prayer. You will first "see it" with eyes of faith, then through what God is doing in other places, and then you will develop the ideas of what to do in your own city. The plan will always include both the conviction that this is what God is leading the church to do and the commitment to Him to do it. As you gain wisdom and experience, the plan will evolve into the perfect plan for your city. I am amazed, however, at how close to the original plan we have remained. Your methods may change somewhat, but the strategy will almost always depend on the original ideas you had for the cell groups.

Scuba Diver's Motto:

"Plan the dive... Dive the plan"

Get Ready and Get Going

Preparation is time well spent, but if it never results in action, it becomes a time waster. So pray, write the vision, set your goals, take the challenge, and develop the plan. But don't just sit there with the paperwork; break ground and break forth. There is much to accomplish.

Chapter 8

Purpose and Values of a Cell Church

Change often kills people's faith in the future. Unable to make any promising connection between a troubled today and a vague tomorrow, they fall into a weary pattern of doubt, cynicism and disillusionment. The organization (church) asks more of everyone, but fails to tie that request to the heartstrings of employees (members). Your job is to justify the struggle, to aim your people toward something special. Never underestimate the power of purpose.[1]

Without a cause, any endeavor becomes mundane and the people's souls go to sleep. To be part of a cause they support, people will sacrifice almost anything they have, even if the cause seems minor or insignificant to the rest of society.

Think of the extreme commitments that people make for animal rights, preservation of historical buildings, restrictions on nuclear power plants, and for the conservation of virgin forests. Many lives have been poured into such causes. Often it seems famous people become bored with their lives and take up causes that may not make much sense to the rest of us. But for the cause, they will jeopardize all that they have and stand for.

What is the motivating force behind this kind of extreme self-sacrifice? PURPOSE. Purpose gives meaning to life. Having purpose says, "I live for something greater than myself." Purpose is the life of any organization. It accomplishes more than the promise of a paycheck, more than personal promotion, and more than fame.

It could be that under these conditions you consider commitment to be a hopeless case. Act otherwise. Too much respect for problems kills our faith in possibilities.[2]

---

[1] Price Pritchett, *Firing Up Commitment During Organizational Change*, Pritchett and Associates, p. 5.
[2] *Ibid.*, p. 25.

Values, Purpose, and Action

Values give meaning to purpose. Once we grasp the purpose of the cell church, we need to understand its values and must begin to teach the congregation the importance of those values. Unless the local church membership internalizes those standards, they will never be able to execute effective cell-church ministry. In addition, for our purposes to be fulfilled, there must be a corresponding action assigned to each purpose.

Before we begin any new venture (such as cell ministry), we should ask ourselves these questions:

What is the greatest desire that I have for ministry?
You must have a burning desire, a craving in your heart to see your mission accomplished.

Do I have God's promise concerning this ministry?
Is God leading you? If this is God's direction in your life and you have His promise, then proceed.

What will I do to see this desire become a reality?
You must be ready to make the commitment to do whatever it takes to see it come to pass.

Whom will I involve in order to accomplish this ministry?
Until you involve other people, you will never see your mission accomplished.

What are my goals and predictions for the success of the ministry?
You must have measurable goals and strong predictions that overcome a negative environment.

What changes am I willing to make to accomplish these goals?
Search your heart and ask God to show you what areas of your life need to change to accomplish the mission.

When will I start?
Carefully set a date, after you are prepared and ready to start on your journey.

The Mission Statement of the Church

It is necessary to have a clear mission statement of your church's purpose. Our mission statement at Bethany is as follows:

> *Bethany World Prayer Center exists to preach the gospel to every person, to pastor believers, to prepare disciples, and to plant leaders around the world.*

Let me break this down for you.

Preach the Gospel

In the cell church, evangelism must be a constant focus. There are several powerful ways that a cell group can effectively preach the Gospel. First, to reach people through the cell groups, each group must pray for the people they want to reach, invite them to cell-group meetings, invite them to other activities besides meetings—such as meals and social gatherings—minister to their felt needs, and show genuine concern for them in various other ways.

Second, the cell group must model true Christianity before others. When cell members live a Christ-like lifestyle, they demonstrate to those around them the true nature of Jesus. This will often stir up questions about faith, and the members can then experience that which is promised in I Peter 3:15. *"But sanctify the Lord God in your hearts: and be ready always to give an answer to every man that asketh you a reason of the hope that is in you with meekness and fear."*

Third, the cell group needs to develop a team mentality for evangelizing their lost friends and relatives. When the entire group is focused on praying for these people and also assists in sharing Christ with them, there can be even more effective results. Often in the groups, the names of "targeted" people are written on a white board. This procedure helps all in the group to be reminded of those for whom they are praying, thereby developing a personal interest in every soul.

Fourth, the final step in preaching the gospel is to have the new convert get water baptized. This is a personal testimony to the convert's salvation experience and gives him or her the *"answer of a good conscience toward God"* (I Peter 3:21).

Pastor Believers

Bringing the new convert into relationship with the local church is one of the greatest challenges that we face. When we are successful in doing so, it becomes one of the greatest blessings to both the new convert and the local church. The first step in pastoring the believer consists of follow-up and assimilation. Assimilation is the process of "connecting" the new convert to the Body of Christ.

The assimilator or assimilation team is responsible to become the connection to the Body for every new believer or visitor to the church. This assimilator does the immediate and long-term follow-up on the converts, whom he meets face to face after the altar call, or on visitors whom he meets after the service. By personal visits, telephone visits, or by inviting the new convert over for fellowship, the assimilator has the opportunity to answer the many questions the person may have.

During the first six weeks of this process, we use a booklet called *Christianity 101* in our discussions with them. It is designed to verify the person's salvation and teach him the importance of regular fellowship in both the cell group and celebration services. It also instructs the person in a simple and effective way to win his loved ones to Christ. Ongoing pastoral care is offered in the group as the new Christian grows in grace and in his personal relationship to Christ.

During the time we are going over the *Christianity 101* booklet with the new convert, we arrange for him to attend the "Encounter Weekend." This life-changing weekend is designed to introduce the person to other Christians and pastors and to ensure that he is set free from personal bondage that would hinder his growth as a Christian. He receives vision for leadership at the retreat and is introduced to the person of the Holy Spirit. Along with this comes instruction concerning the gifts and fruit of the Holy Spirit.

Prepare Disciples

Discipleship is the New Testament method for teaching and training the new Christian in the many aspects of the Christian faith and lifestyle. This includes theological understanding, practical employment of biblical principles, and ministry awareness and skills. Many topics that relate to discipleship are taught at the church in a class called *Discipleship 201*.

The principle of discipleship requires that the new believer be a part of a learning method including active participation in New Testament ministry. His group members and his sponsor, the assimilator, teach him by using both structured methods and less formal training. The new Christian is taught the core values in the life of every Christian. Instruction is given concerning the Person of God and the Word of God. The lordship of Jesus in the believer's life is also taught. The values of family, life, giving, prayer, the local church, and world missions are emphasized. Finally, in the structured teaching, the importance of spiritual authority is covered.

He also learns informally in this new environment because the group models principles of Christ-likeness before him. He is led by the example of his sponsor, and he learns from the group how to discover and deploy spiritual gifts. He observes others applying God's Word to everyday life experiences, and he also discovers the value of being mentored. (More on this later.)

Plant Leaders

The training of leaders locally and around the world is the most important investment of time and energy that the local church can make. Please take a moment to read that statement again and think about it. Is such training being done in your church? How comprehensive is your curriculum for leaders? All potential leaders will require continuing education in many different areas. They must be taught how to build strong relationships and how to communicate effectively within those relationships. Instruction in prayer, intercession, and motivation of others are vital factors in the growth of a leader. Learning to be hospitable and learning how to serve are other important components of leadership development. It is imperative for every leader to be equipped in the skills of planting a new group or a new work and how to effectively pastor and lead that new ministry. To achieve adequate preparation of our leaders, we hold a class at the church called *Leadership 301*. The attendees of this class use a booklet of the same name in their study of effective leadership skills.

Although there are many qualities found in a good leader, seven specific leadership characteristics are necessary:

- First, the leader must exhibit true humility through an attitude of servanthood.

- Second, he must be a person of character, with integrity and an excellent personality.

- Third, spiritual maturity must be evidenced in the life of a true leader.

- Fourth, the person who is a leader must be trustworthy, having earned the confidence of others.

- Fifth, the leader must be of an ethical spirit, living within accepted standards of conduct and morals.

- Sixth, perseverance to overcome the inevitable obstacles and disappointments of life must be demonstrated in a leader.

- Seventh, the true leader lives honestly, earning the respect of his peers.

The ultimate goal of every leader is to reproduce himself and Christ in others. This only happens when every leader is mentored and in turn mentors others. Every leader shares the vision of the local church leadership and works to instill that vision and purpose in all those he personally influences.

Chapter 9

The Mature Church Model

Boudreaux had been ill and had gone to the doctor for a checkup. The doctor ran a series of tests on Boudreaux and told him he would contact him when the results came in. Two weeks later, the doctor phoned Boudreaux and said, "Hey, Boudreaux, I got dem tests back on you!"

Boudreaux answered, "Oh, what did you find out?"

The doctor said, "Well, I got some good news and some bad news for you."

Boudreaux asked, "What's the good news?"

The doctor replied, "You got twenty-four hours to live."

"Twenty-four hours to live?" Boudreaux exclaimed. "Dat's the good news? What's the bad news?"

The doctor answered, "I tried to call you yesterday!"

Sometimes we get hit with a real sense of urgency. We hear the cell-church information, get excited, and want to launch into full-scale cell operation right away. Pray for patience and keep looking toward the mature cell-group churches, who have become successful in winning the lost, as your pattern.

How do we grow up as a church? Let me answer this by suggesting a parallel. Ever see a 40 year-old teenager? Wonder where his or her parents missed it? Like most parents, we are raising our children for the first time, have no experience, and are not sure what the end result should look like. By God's grace, I always had a picture of what my daughters would be as grown-ups. As I guided them through life, I had one goal in mind. The goal was not to raise good "kids," but to raise my kids to be good adults. To do that, I had to have an understanding of what a good adult was like. Thank God there were some good examples around to show us the way.

The same is true of the mature cell-church model. It is imperative that you have a clear picture of what one looks like if you ever expect to be one. The challenge is the same as with children, finding the mature examples to model after.

There are three distinct stages in every ministry: infancy, adolescence, and maturity. Before attaining our goal of becoming a mature cell church, we must first pass through the infant and adolescent stages. During these stages of growth and development, special care must be taken to keep us from straying from the pure model. This chapter will set forth ideals to strive for in our cell-church model.

Follow the Mature Template

It is imperative to have a clear picture of what we want to be in our mature and final state. We cannot just hope that we end up that way; we must *start out with that model!* To do so, however, we must first have a "mature template" that we follow throughout the entire process. For example, a pastor once told me that he wanted to transition into a cell-church ministry, but his groups would start out as "care groups." Another pastor in Tulsa, Oklahoma tried this method of starting out with "infancy" groups (care groups), and they failed miserably. That church has since abandoned the idea of care groups and is now moving ahead into full-scale cell-group ministry. "Just calling them 'care groups' defeated the cell-church concept," the pastor told me. We cannot start out with a program-based concept of cell ministry and expect it to grow into something that it is "genetically" impossible to be. We have to start out with the right model.

When we think of cell ministry, how, exactly, do we picture the final model? Do we know how to groom our church to look like a mature cell church when it is "grown up"? The following traits are characteristics that, I believe, should be present in a mature cell church.

Every Member a Minister

Picture every person in the church as a witness, a counselor, and a servant.

*But speaking the truth in love, may grow up into him in all things, which is the head, [even] Christ: From whom the whole body fitly joined together and compacted by that which **every joint supplieth**, according to the **effectual working in the measure of every part,** maketh increase of the body unto the edifying of itself in love* (Ephesians 4:15-16, emphasis mine).

*And He gave some, apostles; and some, prophets; and some, evangelists; and some, pastors and teachers; for the **perfecting of the saints,** for the **work of the ministry,** for the **edifying of the body of Christ*** (Ephesians 4:11-12, emphasis mine).

According to these Scriptures, the ministry belongs to the saints; therefore, we need to envision a church in which the members are busily carrying out the duties of ministry on a daily basis.

Testimony from a Cell Leader's Weekly Report

God continues to amaze me. The members are starting to realize their gifts and are beginning to operate in them. Praise God, I know that everyone has caught on to the vision of cell groups. I just can't put into words the joy that I have. This is the beginning of the rest of our lives with God. Hallelujah!

All Programs Replaced by Ministry in Cell Groups

The cell-based church should gradually transition every program into the cell structure, if possible. This will produce vibrant, living, reproducing groups that administer the grace of God. Every conceivable ministry that is offered by programs in the church should be transitioned into cell-based ministry. If a program cannot be transferred to the cells, it may be better to let it expire rather than trying to keep it alive. For example, we had a ministry in our church that required personnel to answer phones 24 hours a day. The extra time and manpower needed to keep this program functioning properly were a constant drain on the pastor who was responsible for it. In addition, the program took him away from his cell-group responsibilities. As a result, we eventually terminated the program. Carefully evaluate each program in your church as to its relationship to the cell-group ministry.

All Pastors, Secretaries, Leaders, and Members Doing the Same Thing

Till we all come in the unity of the faith, and of the knowledge of the Son of God, unto a perfect man, unto the measure of the stature of the fullness of Christ (Ephesians 4:13).

When we eliminate competition between departments and programs, we have a much more powerful thrust. Because cell-based ministry offers an inclusive ministry to individuals in our church, we can focus on cell groups and be confident that the needs of every person are being met sufficiently. The power of having every staff person and every church member speaking the same vision and working to achieve it is awesome. It is only since developing the cell-church model at Bethany that I can say that I am confident that all those who get involved in cells will have their needs met. Anyone who comes to me with needs can receive ongoing ministry in a cell group. When the entire church is permeated with this one ministry, there are no conflicting philosophies that can sideline ministry to individuals.

Leaders Raised Up and Engaged in Evangelism and Discipleship

*And the things that thou hast heard of me among many witnesses, the same commit thou to **faithful** men, who shall be **able to teach** others also* (II Timothy 2:2).

In every cell group, ongoing relationship-based discipleship and ministry training are targeted. Mentored by their cell leaders and the leaders that oversee them, potential leaders progress from one level of training to another. This modeling of leadership by the mentor shows the prospective leader exactly what he will be doing when he himself takes a cell group. Leaders thrive under this type of training, as they personally perform what they see their mentors doing. Also, evangelism and discipleship skills are more easily transmitted in this way.

A Growing Leadership Base

Leaders raising up leaders for a multiplying base of cell groups is our method for reaching our city for Christ. A growing leadership base will eventually result in a cell group being located in every subdivision of the city, led by a trained individual with the same vision and purpose as the pastor and his staff. The broader our leadership base, the more people we can pastor effectively, and the greater influence we will have in our city. The result is that we will reach more people and care for more people as our leaders replicate themselves in others.

A Highly Developed Model That Can Be Reproduced

In order to achieve our goal of a mature cell church, we must develop a predictable system that will ensure success but will still allow the Holy Spirit to move freely. It must be a system that fully utilizes the many different kinds of people in our churches, capitalizing on their different gifts, temperaments, and backgrounds. In addition, each component of the system must be simple, easy to learn, and predictable. We cannot expect people to create their own cell groups or ministries and automatically assume that a large percentage will be successful. We must give them a specific, successful system to follow. (Example: There is an 80% failure rate for small, independently operated businesses compared to an 80% success rate for franchise stores with proven systems.)[1]

This is challenging stuff! But with a proven system, we can expect to have an 80% or better success rate. We will have to create a "cookie cutter" model that can be reproduced anywhere in our area. This model will exhibit the unique personality of the people who are involved in each individual group, but will, nevertheless, function the same in every group. By following this well-defined model, reproduction will occur endless numbers of times until our city is saturated with cell groups that are part of a predictable system in which the Holy Spirit can still move freely.

Support and Encouragement

To achieve maturity in our cell church and to involve the major percentage of the congregation, we must provide the opportunity for people to easily become involved in successful ministry. The mature cell church provides a way for people with a heart to serve and a willingness to be trained to enter into such ministry. After all, people don't need a degree in theology to become cell leaders; they need experience with God and with other people. With the full support of the pastoral staff and other leaders in the cell-group system, the average person can function quite successfully in a cell setting. This makes ministry accessible and provides a two-way accountability structure.

---

[1] Michael Gerber, *The E-Myth Revisited*, Harper Collins Publishers, Inc., New York, New York, 1995, p.82.

A Productive Staff

Through the cell ministry, we will soon have a staff that is working harder than ever before, but *enjoying* their work more. Focused on their goals and ministries, the entire staff should be working at being the best that they can possibly be in cell-group ministry. They will have no dead space in their week while they wait for another church meeting; instead, they will be busily involved with the people in their area of responsibility, caring for them and keeping them healthy.

A Ministry That Produces Consistent Results

In our mature cell-church model, our desire is for a ministry that produces consistent results for not only the cell member but also for the leaders, the pastoral staff, and the lost people in the city. If we have developed a clearly defined structure that can ensure a measure of success, most people will gladly cooperate with us. A system that takes into account the varying degrees of education, intelligence, and ability of people, yet produces results for all, excites people as they realize that, with basic training and instruction, God can use them, too. With the Holy Spirit as our guide, we work within an uncomplicated structure to which most people can successfully adapt.

Every Member Operating in the Gift of God

Many churches are constantly engaged in a "talent search" for capable workers, yet their congregations are already full of God-gifted people. Some churches have created a model that restricts ministry involvement to a few "bright stars" instead of empowering the masses. Doesn't the Bible say that the leaders are to equip the saints to do the work of the ministry? Let's not forget who are the saints. Cell groups open up many ministry opportunities for those saints—believers—who want to get involved.

I will never forget an incident that opened my eyes to the gift of God in people. Lucille Anderson, an elderly grandmother in our church, approached me early on in our cell ministry and asked if she could do a monolog during our first district get-together. I was reluctant. This was the first big meeting of all of the people in my district, and I wanted to impress them with the cell-group ministry that was being developed for them. I expected five to six hundred people to attend and really didn't want to take any chances with doing something that might have a negative reflection on our cells.

But, Lucille was a sweet lady and I just couldn't say no! So, I arranged for her to do her monolog for me the Wednesday night before the district meeting to make sure that everything would be all right. I didn't expect much. Man, was I surprised!

Lucille showed up and shared with me that many of her relatives had died of cancer. She had also contracted cancer and was given no hope by the doctors. She explained how the Lord had given her the verses of scripture that told the story of the woman with the issue of blood, who pushed her way through the crowd just to "touch the hem of His garment."

Lucille then proceeded to reenact this biblical drama before my eyes. As she played the part of this hopeless woman, she threw herself on the floor of the office and began to cry out, "Oh, if I could just touch the hem of His garment, I know I will be healed." This was really a reenactment of her own testimony of how God healed her from cancer. I could not control the tears as I witnessed the incredible gifts of God that Lucille possessed— not only of healing, but also of drama, as she demonstrated the amazing grace of God.

Lucille performed at our district meeting, and at the end the people all jumped to their feet and began to praise God. There was not a dry eye in the building that night.

We must have faith that the gifts that the Holy Spirit has deposited in all believers will help them to function effectively in the Kingdom of God. Consider this Scripture:

Wherefore I put thee in remembrance that thou stir up the gift of God, which is in thee by the putting on of my hands (II Timothy 1:6).

There had been, apparently, some communication on Timothy's part to Paul concerning criticism of his youth and, perhaps, even his handling of situations in the church. The answer that the apostle gave transcends formal training and practical experience. Paul said, "stir up the gift." Whether that gift is serving, evangelism, management, or compassion, it needs to be stirred up and utilized in the local church on a cell-group level.

The gift of God in every believer can bring effective ministry results.

As every man hath received the gift, [even so] minister the same one to another, as good stewards of the manifold grace of God (I Peter 4:10).

It is by the power of God's gift to every man that we are to minister. We minister "the same" to one another. This is further evidence of the importance that Scripture gives to the operation of spiritual and ministry gifts in the life of **every** believer.

The "Fire of God"

I've asked the pastors in Bogotá and in Solo, Indonesia, to what one thing they contribute their great success. Both answered, "Fire!" Fire is the presence of the Holy Spirit that purges us of the distractions of this world and allows us to burn with desire for the things of God. How do we get it?

PRAY, PRAY, PRAY!

As we pass through the transition process, we must endeavor to keep our goals and the model of a mature cell church ever before us. As we make decisions, we must base them on what we want our "finished product" to look like and how we want it to function. If we don't compromise in the process, and if we *pray, pray, pray,* we will end up with a mature, vibrant cell church.

Chapter 10

Reaching Your Personal Community

It is commonplace that the main theme of Acts is the work of the Holy Spirit, and that He is the supreme agent in the Christian mission. Yet this is the very factor which is most often forgotten in assessing conversion in the early Church. The Christians were convinced that the Spirit of Jesus had come into their midst and indwelt their very personalities in order to equip them for evangelism, for making Him known to others. Acts is the story, seen from one apostolic man's perspective, of how this was worked out.[1]

Taking the Gospel to the world, one person at a time.

*And this gospel of the kingdom shall be **preached in all the world** for a witness unto all nations; and then shall the end come* (Matthew 24:14).

In this verse, *world* is the Greek word *oikoumene*. It means "every inhabited dwelling." During the time of the Roman Empire when the word *oikoumena* was used, the term referred to **every** subject in the Empire. If Caesar wanted to deliver a message to the entire Roman Empire, soldiers went to every home, house by house, thus delivering the message to every person in the Empire.

If we take that same idea of the necessity of every house receiving this vital news of the Gospel, then as Christians, we have an obligation in our time to see that every inhabited dwelling receives the Gospel of Christ before He returns. There is no other way to guarantee that the Gospel is truly preached to all the world except through house-to-house ministry. When we penetrate a subdivision or a city or a section of our city, we can know that we have gone to every house and have attempted to reach our city.

---

[1] Michael Green, *Evangelism in the Early Church*, Eagle, Guildford, Surrey, U.K., 1970, p. 178.

Although both television and radio are important in spreading the Gospel, mass media alone does not ensure that every home is receiving the message of Christ. Many individuals around the world do not have access to radios or televisions. Other people who do own televisions or radios don't tune in to Christian programming. But all people everywhere in the world have a dwelling of one kind or another, even if it's only a cardboard box in a New York City alley. Therefore, if we assume the responsibility of going into every "home" with the Gospel, we can be sure that we are reaching the world for Christ.

The Ministry of the Evangelist

Once we accept the importance of bringing the Gospel to every home, the next question is "Who should go?" That is the work of an evangelist. The evangelist is the one who is supposed to go into all the world. At this point, however, our usual way of thinking is challenged.

During a cell-group seminar, I once asked a group of people, "What is your idea of an evangelist?" Many responded with answers such as, "a strong, outgoing person," "one who shouts and beats on the pulpit," "someone who preaches judgment if you don't repent," "a person who has a love for the lost," and "someone who is here today and gone tomorrow." One man said, "He is a spiritual terrorist!"

Then I asked another question: "What kind of person led you to Christ?" I now received totally different answers, such as "she was gentle, not pushy," "real," "full of joy, truth, and Jesus," and "he was patient, always there for me."

The true evangelist is not the one who blows in, blows up, and then blows out. Instead, he is the one who has built a relationship with you and paid the price in prayer to win you to Christ. He is the person who was always there for you, patiently ministering to you with longsuffering and love. That definition encompasses every person in the Body of Christ who is willing to reach his/her relative, neighbor, or friend for Christ.

When Paul told Timothy to *"do the work of an evangelist"* (II Timothy 4:5), I don't think he meant for Timothy to get on the road with a "Holy Ghost revival tent" and start itinerating in all the churches. I believe he meant for Timothy to build meaningful relationships with people in his city in order to win them to Christ. The itinerating revivalist still has his place in the church of Jesus Christ, but the definition and ministry of the evangelist is not limited to this traditional understanding of the weekend revival preacher.

C. Peter Wagner, in his book *Finding Your Spiritual Gifts,* writes that between 5% and 10% of Christians have the **gift** of evangelism. But we know that Christ calls us all to be laborers in the harvest, and by *His* grace, we can be.

What Is an *Oikos?*

In Acts 16:15, the Bible points out that *"she [Lydia] was baptized, and her household (oikos)."* The Bible says in Acts 16:34 that the prison keeper *"rejoiced, believing in God with all his house (oikos)."* In Acts 18:8, Crispus *"believed on the Lord with all his house (oikos)."* In those days, a household included not only a man's wife and children, but his servants as well.

The Greek word *oikos* refers to your personal community, which is primarily your family, immediate and distant. Your extended *oikos* includes not only your friends and neighbors, but also the people with whom you come in contact on a daily or weekly basis. Those you encounter at work, at the store, at a favorite restaurant, or at any other place you frequent on a regular basis would then be part of your extended *oikos.*

Your neighbor – *Plesion*

Testimony of Betty Franklin

About 40 or 50 people attended the 'Neighborhood Outreach' that we planned in our community. Thirteen of those people gave their hearts to the Lord! We prepared food and gave toys to the needy. The cell members gave their personal testimonies of what the Lord had done in their lives. During the outreach we ministered to the needs of those who were going through tough times.

We have followed-up those who gave their life to the Lord by weekly phone calls, encouraging them to visit our cell group where they can be in an atmosphere of love, acceptance, and accountability, and where they can grow to be all that God intends for them to be.

The vision for our cell group is to bring the neighborhood into a relationship with Jesus Christ, the local church, and each other.

In the New Testament, the word *plesion* (Greek for *neighbor*) refers to those relationships outside your *oikos* community. In the parable of the Good Samaritan, we get a clear meaning of the word *plesion*. Luke 10:36-37 says, *"Which now of these three, thinkest thou, was neighbour unto him that fell among the thieves? And he said, He that shewed mercy on him. Then said Jesus unto him, Go, and do thou likewise."* From this Scripture we see that it is our choice to "shew mercy" to all those with whom we come in contact. When we show mercy to people, we become their *plesion* and may eventually win them to Christ.

We need to understand how the *oikos* principle of evangelism can enable us to reach untold numbers of souls. The whole world is built on these webs of relationships that are somehow networked together through personal communities. I believe that God has designed it that way so the number of people to whom we are related and can reach never ends. There is, however, a limited group that we relate to on an ongoing and consistent basis.

A family is a perfect example of this type of networking. My own parents raised six children, five boys and one girl. My brothers, sister, and I had uncles, aunts, cousins and grandparents. Later when each of us married, we created in-laws. When I married, I thought I was marrying just my wife; but, in effect, I married her family, too. All her aunts, uncles, cousins, and grandparents were now a part of my extended family. Every time one of my in-laws married, a person I hadn't known before became my children's uncle or aunt. Before long, there was a mass of people to whom I could reach out. I recently counted all the people in my *oikos* who have given their hearts to Christ. To my joy and amazement, I counted **forty** souls!

We need to realize that God has brought our extended family into our lives, and we should take every opportunity to reach every one of them. These people may have been waiting for years for someone to share the Gospel with them. Through this endless group of people, this *oikos,* we can evangelize for the rest of our lives. We can effectively fulfill the Great Commission. We don't have to go "street preaching" to get people saved. All we have to do is work within our personal community, faithfully reaching out to people whom we already know. This is the most natural and effective way to reach "our" world for Christ.

Jesus' Example

Jesus was called *"a friend of publicans and sinners"* (Matthew 11:19). He made it His business to reach sinners. For example, Zacchaeus was a sinner, a wicked man; yet, Jesus chose to eat lunch with him one day. Luke 19:5 says, *"And when Jesus came to the place, He looked up and saw him, and said unto him, 'Zacchaeus, make haste and come down; for to day I must abide at thy house.'"* Jesus invited Himself over to Zacchaeus' house, then penetrated his *oikos* and by doing so, reached him with salvation. Like Jesus, we have to learn how to penetrate the *oikos* and the extended personal communities of unbelievers in our lives.

Ways to Penetrate *Oikoi*

In the United States, eighty million people work or volunteer in some civic or non-profit organization. When a person joins any one of these organizations, there is immediate acceptance. I remember a time when I called one of these groups. By the time I got off the phone, a man had accepted me, invited me to a meeting, and was going to send my membership card and an envelope for the first year's membership dues. If I had gone to a meeting, there would have been another fifty to one hundred people who would have accepted me immediately. This was a secular organization that could easily be penetrated by Christians who were willing to establish relationships and lead others in the organization to Christ. No matter where you live or how new you are to the community, you can have an immediate *oikos* to penetrate.

Through the power of the Holy Spirit, God has given us influence. Whether we realize it or not, we influence people's lives. They will either run from us, or they will be attracted to us. When we wholeheartedly serve God, people will observe how we handle tragedy with power, composure, and the Holy Spirit's guidance, comfort, and peace. Our actions can make an impact on them, gaining us access into their lives to further minister to them by our God-given influence.

After we become Christians, we are usually surrounded by Christian friends. Whether consciously or not, from that point on we tend to isolate ourselves from the lost. Can you see how this would diminish our useful-ness to the Kingdom of God? Time and again I have seen this isolation eventually carry over to our church involvement, and we stop caring for one another's needs.

Cell-group ministry, however, allows us to become involved with what God is doing in the earth today. Cell groups are not only groups that care for the sheep, but they are also evangelistic, multiplying, praying-type groups. After strengthening each other in our cells, we need to look at the fields of harvest made ready by the Lord of the Harvest. Then, as a team, we help each other, working together to reach the lost people in our rela-tionships and drawing them into God's kingdom.

Divine Appointments

Testimony of Vera Blakes

> *Three cell groups from our zone came together to be a blessing in the community. Our plan was to clean a yard, but God knew that there was more to do! Mrs. Guidroz's floor furnace was not work-ing, and the temperatures had been in the low 30's. While the men and children cleaned the yard, one of our ladies called her husband (who is not a cell member) to come and fix the furnace. While all of this was taking place, one of the cell members who is very tenderhearted visited with Mrs. Guidroz, who is blind. She spoke comforting words of understanding to this dear lady who was still grieving over the death of a brother.*
>
> *God has a plan for each one of us to touch a life. Some came to cut trees and sack and haul, others to sing praises and pray. Some came to bring warmth to a cold house, still others to comfort and be available for God's purpose. All came to show the love of Jesus in action!*

In addition to your *oikos*, The Holy Spirit provides divine appointments. I believe the Holy Spirit actually arranges more divine appointments than we can ever imagine. How many times have we run across someone with whom we later wished we had shared Christ? Maybe God even told us to say something, but we didn't. These are divine appointments.

On a plane headed for Germany one day, a big guy who worked in the South China Sea on an oil rig came up to me and said, "Hey, what's going on? Your face is all lit up. There is something about you that is different." I told him, "Sit down. It's Jesus that is different about me." I began to share with him all that God had done for me in my life. Then I said, "Look, if you need any help, call me or write me and let me know." I gave him my address in Germany.

About three months later, I received a letter from this man. He said, "You may not remember me, but I met you on flight such and such going to Germany. I just want you to know there's a new baby Christian out in the South China Sea." He had given his heart to Christ!

We need to recognize and appreciate the divine appointments that God is setting up all around us.

Prayer Triplets

To persuade people to come to a cell group, a strategy must be devised. One systematic plan to accomplish this is a method called "Prayer Triplets." Developed by Dr. Karen Hurston,[2] this teaching on prayer for the lost has been applied to our cell-group ministry. According to Dr. Hurston, Christians should come together and share the names of three friends, relatives, or other members of their *oikos* or extended *oikoi*. This gives each person some target people to pray for and reach out to for salvation. This has been effective in targeting those relatives and friends whom we feel are closest to coming to Christ. A five-step plan that can be easily applied to implement this stategy is what I call Project E-I-E-I-O.

Testimony from a Cell Leader's Weekly Report

Praise God! After fellowship we went into praise and worship. The power of God fell. It was like a mighty wind as God began to touch people's lives. Some began to cry and some just fell in His presence. Later we began discussion and ministered to one another. Before the meeting was over, a visitor gave his life to the Lord! We all rejoiced at what God had done because his family was one of the ones we had been praying for!

---

[2] Shared by Dr. Hurston in a staff seminar during Bethany World Prayer Center's transition to cells.

Old MacDonald Has an *Oikos*, E- I - E - I - O!

- **Encircle** — The first step in E-I-E-I-O is to **ENCIRCLE** the target people with prayer. *Encircle* means "to surround; to form a circle around." Praying in this way pulls down walls of demonic obstruction, spiritual blindness, and diversion in the lives of the target people. We begin to pray protection, safety, and trust around them. When an element of trust develops, the ones for whom we have been praying will open up to us without feeling intimidated or resentful. Our boldness to approach them with the Gospel thus increases, making it easier to share with them.

Once we start praying for our target people, we will find that love and compassion will pour out of us for that person. The expression of our increased concern will then cause the person to respond positively. The door opens further because prayer breaks down resistance. The Bible says, *"The fervent, effectual prayer of a righteous man availeth much"* (James 5:16). The Greek word for effectual actually means "boiling over." It denotes a situation that is both intensive and hot, like Cajun food (our local cuisine). Prayer can also be described as effectual in that it accomplishes the desired task. We read this in James, *"ye have not, because ye ask not. Ye ask and receive not, because ye ask amiss"* (4:2b,3). When we are praying according to the heart of God—for the salvation of the lost—we know He hears and answers our prayers. (See 1 John 5:14,15.)

Intercessory warfare-type prayer achieves spiritual purposes. When we know a person's problem, what his needs are, and what his obstacles are, we can pray after that fashion. We can pray fervently against the attack of the enemy on that person. As we pray for God's intervention in his life and spend time in earnest prayer for him, we will see a change.

- **Invite** — The second thing we do is to **INVITE** one of the target people to spend time with us. Invite means "to ask for the presence of that person at a place or a gathering, providing an opportunity for something to happen; to request formally; to welcome; encourage."[3] We want to allow a chance for the Holy Spirit to do something in that person's

---

[3] Throughout this section the definitions have been supplied by *The Living Webster Encyclopedic Dictionary*, published by the English Language Institute of America in Chicago, 1975.

life; thus, during this lunch, golf game, or shopping outing, we should look for an opportunity to interject God's answer to one of his problems, or share a testimony with him. We may want to take the opportunity to share about the blessings of God in our own life. This doesn't have to be a sermon; in fact, a sermon is hardly ever appropriate in such situations. But whatever we share, we need to make sure that the occasion has a spiritual element, otherwise there will be no resulting spiritual fruit.

After the initial outing, invite the person to a cell group. This allows the person to get acquainted with other Christians in a non-threatening environment. As he meets other people, he develops a built-in spiritual support system for the time when he is ready to accept Christ.

After visiting the cell group, the person will be much more open to visiting the church. When he actually visits the church, he will already have relationships with people there and will be familiar with some of the terminology. Things will not seem so new and foreign to him, and he will be able to be receptive to the work of the Holy Spirit in his life.

- **Enlist** — Because we've been praying for this person to come out of darkness and into light, the Holy Spirit begins to deal with him, and our words penetrate his hard, outer shell. As we persist in prayer and invitations, the day will come when he will open himself to salvation. After he has made his decision for the Lord, we are ready to implement the third part of our plan, that is, to **ENLIST** him in the Kingdom of God. The word *enlist* means "to engage (person or persons) for service in the armed forces." New believers thus become soldiers in God's army. But as a newborn babe in Christ, he will need care. This brings us to the next step of our process.

- **Intern** — The fourth step is to intern the newly enlisted babe in Christ. To **INTERN** means "to work to gain practical experience, just as a graduate of medical school serves his internship at a hospital, learning how to put into practice what he has learned in school." In the Christian context, the intern process is called discipleship. Every new believer needs someone to help walk him through the practical steps of Christianity. Through the mentor/protege relationship on the cell-group level, discipleship is accomplished.

As people come to a saving knowledge of the Lord Jesus, we desire for them to learn how to live and abide in Christ and how to mature as believers. It is important for a new believer to learn how to bless instead of curse, how to pray for those who despitefully use him, how to face sin and overcome it, how to hear the voice of God, and how to understand the Scriptures. The process of internship takes the new believer from being a totally dependent child to becoming a mature adult who cares for others. It brings his salvation from being a great and glorious single experience to becoming a God-glorifying and victorious lifestyle.

- **Obligate** — During the course of the internship process, the last step of our plan is implemented. It is now time to **OBLIGATE** the person. To obligate means "to bind, compel, or constrain by a social, legal, or moral tie." At this point in time, help the person to understand his responsibility before God to reach his own *oikos* and extended *oikos*. The revelation that he is the best person to reach his own family and friends will have to be put into his heart by God, just as He has placed that awareness in the hearts of most Christians. But when that realization comes, encourage him to step forward to fulfill his role in the "Great Commission" to preach the Gospel to all the world.

With obligation birthed into the heart of the new believer, E-I-E-I-O is now completed. The target person was first encircled with prayer, then invited to gatherings for spiritual input. Upon salvation, the new convert was enlisted into the Kingdom of God and effectively discipled through the internship process. Finally, the new believer accepted the obligation of reaching into his own circle of influence with the Gospel message, and, from that point, the process begins anew. By embracing the simple evangelistic principles of *oikos* penetration, we can realize the master plan that God has established for the harvesting of souls.

Chapter 11

How Does It Function on Cell Night?

At the seafood outlet called Tony's Seafood on Plank Road in Baton Rouge, there are more kinds of seafood than you can imagine. The store is full of catfish, redfish, grouper, boiled crawfish and shrimp, and many other Cajun delicacies. In one corner of the store is the deli where you can buy delicious "boudin balls." These are made of pork meat mixed with Cajun spices, onions, and rice all rolled up and deep-fried to perfection.

One day Boudreaux had bought a bag of boudin balls. He was standing outside the store eating them when Thibodeaux walked by and asked, "Boudreaux, what you got there, eh?"

Boudreaux replied, "I got me some boudin balls."

Thibodeaux asked, "Boudreaux, why don't you give me one of dem boudin balls?"

Boudreaux said, "Thiboudeaux, if you guess how many boudin balls I got in that bag, I'll give you both of them!"

After a few minutes of thinking, Thibodeaux answered, "Five!"

How are you at interpreting data? Sometimes, like Thibodeaux, the conclusions we come to don't really add up. This is especially true for leaders who are trying to guess why people stop going to their cell-group meetings. The truth is sometimes a total surprise. A relative of mine had attended a cell group meeting for several weeks and then just stopped going. I asked him why he wasn't attending cell group any more. His answer shocked me, but did not surprise me. He said, "The whole time the meeting is going on, the leaders let their grandchildren play on the floor in the middle of the group circle. It is so distracting that I can't concentrate on the lesson, so I just quit going to the group!"

"We never seem to get to the lesson, we just sing all night!" "The leader is never prepared and the group has no direction." "The meeting lasts too long!"

These are all good reasons that sincere people give as to why they drop out of cell groups. Before we start blaming leaders, let's realize that leadership training, specific to cell groups, is essential. In this chapter we'll look at some tips for leaders that may help them reduce "member drop-out." There is a right way to hold a meeting and some negatives that you need to avoid. Look at the following format for a successful cell-group meeting.

Bathe the Meeting in Prayer

Without prayer, no specific format for a cell-group meeting will ensure success. Only prayer can make meetings life-giving experiences that keep people coming back for more. Without prayer, cell groups will be laborious and frustrating, like every other plan of man in the church. Therefore, before any format can be effective, a "Gideon's Army" of prayer warriors must be actively supporting the cell effort in the church. Assuming that prayer is first laid as a foundation, we have found that groups that follow the format explained in this chapter have proven to be the most consistently successful groups.

Three Goals of the Meeting

- **Fellowship** — The initial goal of the cell meeting is to set at ease all members and visitors through fellowship. I will define fellowship as relaxed conversation during which we are discovering common interests and purposes. Fellowship begins with the welcome at the door then continues by befriending visitors through conversation and by helping them to relax through sharing refreshments and laughing together.

- **Encouragement** — We edify people by providing support, guidance, and affirmation. This "building up" is essential in the success of the cell meeting because it stimulates the good feeling that is necessary to make people open to ministry and to bring them back time and again. Other ways to encourage people include embracing them as friends, giving them timely instruction in the Scriptures, and imparting vision for their lives in the purposes of God.

- **Meeting needs** — Everyone has needs. We meet these for cell members when we take the time to listen carefully to their concerns, then respond with practical solutions and help. At the end of the discussion time, it is very important to break into smaller sub-groups in which you can facilitate openness and minister more effectively. (These sub-groups are usually arranged by gender or specific need.) Affirmation of the individual is also an important part of the need-meeting process. Remember, it is not the work you do, it is the service you render.

Now let's look at how the cell meeting is organized and how it generally functions.

Before the Meeting Starts

The best time to plan next week's meeting is during this week's meeting. The most appropriate time seems to be as the **fellowship time** at the beginning of the meeting is winding down. Take about ten minutes then to plan the next meeting. Where is the meeting going to be held? Who is going to lead it? These are obvious decisions that need to be made. If there will be any snacks and there *should* be (my personal motto is that stressed spelled backwards is *desserts!*), decide who will bring what and also decide who will be watching the children at the meeting. Childcare is an important ministry in and of itself, particularly when it is a shared ministry. If childcare is planned well in advance, the person providing the care for that week can arrive early and have something prepared for the children. Failure to plan childcare and activities for the children, however, can create real problems.

For instance, one night we were at a cell group and one woman was especially excited about being at the meeting. She had her notebook on her lap, pen in hand, and was all ready to take notes. One minute before the meeting was to start, however, the cell leader asked her if she would watch the children. I saw her excited countenance turn into one of disappointment as she closed her books and got up to watch the kids. She wasn't prepared and couldn't offer the children her best. What if she had needed personal ministry that night? Because that cell leader didn't plan in advance, this lady may have missed her blessing and ministry from God, and the children missed out on what could have been a powerful time for them. A little advance planning would have made for a much better meeting.

During the planning time for the next meeting, you will also need to decide how praise and worship will be handled, whether to use a guitar, play the piano, or use cassette tapes. Most of our cells use tapes, but we have also provided training for the cell leaders so that they can more easily lead worship in their meetings.

After the planning meeting and before the next meeting, the cell leader and intern should plan for and study the lesson. The lesson is picked up the week before the meeting at the district office at church. (Every cell group is assigned to a district that has a physical office at the church facility.) As they study the lesson together, they should write down their ideas. Then when the time for the meeting arrives, both the cell leader and the intern will be familiar with the lesson and have something to share.

Prayer and fasting should be as much a part of planning for the meeting as studying the lesson. We ask our cell leaders to pray an hour every day for their cell members and to fast the day of the meeting, if possible. If a cell group seems to struggle a little bit with the meetings or with follow-up, the leadership should go back to prayer and fasting, and they will soon see a great change.

Meeting Time

Getting Started

A clean house and a warm smile should greet everyone attending the meeting that night. Cleanliness and friendliness are the beginning of a successful meeting. Once, at a seminar I was holding, I asked a group of people how they would define hospitality. Some of their answers were,

"Make people feel welcome or special," "Make people feel comfortable and at home, loved, and accepted," "Be kind and open, extend yourself, go out of your way, go the extra mile for guests," and *"Make your best available to them."* Webster's dictionary defines hospitality as a *"cordial and generous reception of or disposition toward guests."*

The host of the cell meeting should never be busy doing last minute tasks (such as vacuuming) while the guests are standing in the living room not doing anything. Instead, the attention of the host should be given totally to his guests. There is nothing worse than to be invited to someone's home if the person who invited you is so busy that he doesn't have time to talk with you for the first half hour.

Always make people feel they are valued guests and truly welcome in your home. If you do, they will never forget your kindness and hospitality. Hebrews 6:10 says, *"For God is not unrighteous to forget your work and labour of love, which ye have shewed toward his name, in that ye have ministered to the saints, and do minister."* When we are hospitable, we are making cell members and visitors feel as if they are the most important people on earth.

Hospitality doesn't have to be fancy or expensive, but it should be an offering from the heart. I've talked to missionaries who have been in natives' homes where they were given another family member's portion to eat. In fact, missionaries who visited in Romania told me they were guests in homes where the family members would fight over the privilege of giving up their own meal for the guest to eat. Never forget sacrifice, and be willing yourself to sacrifice for others.

As guests arrive, direct them to the area of the house where others are gathering. Don't let people walk into a "meeting" atmosphere, which is cold and unnatural. Rather, let them walk into a relaxed time of fellowship. Informal fellowship is necessary because it breaks down many walls. It warms up visitors to the members of the cell group, enabling the visitors to see that the cell members are normal people. Above all, avoid the appearance of a cultist group; be natural in your fellowship.

Worship

Your group worship time can actually usher the group into the very presence of God, preparing everyone's heart to receive from Him. Do keep in mind that the cell group's worship time will be different from a larger church worship service. That's as it should be. There isn't a need for half an hour or an hour of worship, especially if unsaved guests are present. Worship for only eight to ten minutes, and be sensitive to the fact that many visitors will not know the songs. Select songs that are exciting, that edify people, and that exalt the Lord. At Bethany, we have developed "sing-a-long" cassette tapes with song sheets to help in the area of worship. This practice will vary from group to group, but let the intimate atmosphere bless your fellowship together.

The Icebreaker

After worship, introduce the visitors and do an icebreaker. An icebreaker is a simple question that helps the conversation get started. The icebreaker needs to be fun and exciting, but not childish. The question can relate to the lesson but doesn't have to. One example of a good icebreaker might be "What was your favorite pet as a child?" One week I did a lesson on finances, and the icebreaker was "What object besides your home and car have you spent the most money on in your life? Was it worth it and why?" The icebreaker question should not be too threatening (as in too personal) or else people will be reluctant to participate, and the purpose of the cell meeting is to get people to open up. In one meeting, the icebreaker was "What was the worst thing that ever happened in your life?" That threw a wet blanket over everything. It was a terrible icebreaker.

An icebreaker should begin with the cell leader answering the question, then every person, going either clockwise or counter-clockwise, takes a turn answering. Encourage participation at this more relaxed time because if someone doesn't say anything during the icebreaker, chances are that he won't say anything during the discussion part of the meeting. Urge everyone to say something, but don't let the icebreaker take up the whole meeting. The cell leader needs to be responsible for how long people share. He could start off by saying, "O.K., you have 30 to 60 seconds to answer." After the time limit, he should just say, "Well, time's up. Next."

Childcare

It is the responsibility of everyone in the group, not just the parents, to care for the children. The parents won't ever be a part of the meeting if  they just come over to babysit their own children. Consequently, all the cell members will have to share and sacrifice a little for these parents to make sure that they receive ministry. For those with newborns, you may have to offer separate babysitting.

After the worship, the children can be dismissed to another room to see a Christian video, play a game, or view some printed material designed for children. (We have prepared children's object lessons for each week's meeting.) Only about thirty to forty minutes of actual activity will be needed because that's how long the adult discussion period should be. Provide the children with object lessons and short projects with a spiritual theme that allow them to interact with one another. Be creative with the children. At the end of the discussion period, and after the adults have prayed, bring the children back into the cell meeting and pray with them.

Some children may be mature enough to participate in the cell group. This allows them to see their parents respond to God in a positive way and might be the best thing that ever happened to them as a Christian family.

Facilitate and Discuss

It may take some time, but learn how to be a good facilitator. Learn how to keep the discussion going. After worship, immediately proceed to the Scripture reference and to the discussion period. At this time it is not necessary that each person give an answer. *Openness and liberty is the key.* In other words, there should be an even interchange of the discussion topic, going back and forth between the people present.

We want everyone to answer spontaneously, but if only two people are answering all the questions, a problem exists. This is where a good facilitator comes in. If the same person raises his hand for every question, the facilitator should say, "Let's have someone else answer this time." The first few times that the cell leader intervenes in this way might be difficult, but he will eventually get the hang of it. It might seem a little rude to tell someone to let others speak, but it is just as rude to others if we don't let them talk. We can't force other people to say anything, but we should always give them opportunities to talk. Besides, those who love to talk are going to talk whether they are called on or not.

Be sensitive to what others confide in you regarding their abilities or lack thereof. I knew a lady one time who could not read. She confided to her cell-group leader, "I can't read, so please don't call on me to read the Scriptures." Don't you know that every time they met as a group, the leader would say, "Sister, would you read this next verse for us?" She quit going to that cell group.

On another occasion, a pastor had the habit of asking other people in the church to close in prayer. One man told the pastor privately that he just couldn't speak in public, so he wanted the pastor to respect this by never calling on him to close the service in prayer. Sure enough, a few months later, the pastor turned to him at the end of the service and asked, "Brother, would you close in prayer?" The man stood up and said angrily, "Now I told you not to call on me!" I feel the pastor deserved that rebuke, didn't he? (And it wasn't me!) Encourage involvement and participation, but never put people on the spot.

The Leader Must Listen

The cell leader is responsible to keep the discussion intense. Intensity keeps things interesting, and if it's not interesting, people won't come back. Try sitting on the edge of a chair, leaning forward, and bringing the people into the discussion. Look every cell member in the eyes while addressing them. Nod your head in agreement or in acknowledgment of what members say.

Invite their input by asking specific questions such as, "Joe, how was your week?" "What one thing did you learn from last week's meeting?" Ask for clarification. Comment on the feeling behind the words used. "This seems to have really affected you…" Expressing loving concern protects members' confidences. "This has been a trial for you. Let's pray for God's help." Don't criticize with, "You know you need to get over this," or even inappropriate humor at their expense, "Get a life!"

This carries over to all times that we should listen to others. I have been guilty of shortchanging people myself in the matter of paying attention to their words. Has this ever happened to you? I've been in the middle of answering an email when someone has entered my office. I stop typing and start listening to what they're telling me, but my eyes keep drifting back to my email. Finally I start typing again and I tell them, "Keep talking. I'm still listening." The truth is "I ain't listening!" They're talking, but I am not really listening. We need to give others our full attention, and this is particularly crucial in cell-group meetings.

Good Small-Group Dynamics

It is important for each cell leader to understand and implement good small-group dynamics. Understanding good small-group dynamics increases the effectiveness of the group's discussion time. This can have a powerful effect in the lives of those involved. Here are some basic guidelines and tips that will enhance the cell leader's role as facilitator.

General Guidelines

- All members share equally in the ownership of the meeting. Anyone can share.

- The group will follow a two-week format, alternating from body ministry (edification) to outreach for unbelievers (evangelism). This allows for a variety of subject matter that is always interesting.

- Sharing will follow the general rules of brevity, appropriateness, and courtesy. No one is to dominate the discussion. We will speak openly and honestly.

- We will help keep the interaction in line with what Christ is doing in our midst and refrain from storytelling that is irrelevant to the subject being discussed.

- When speaking, we will address the group and not just the leader.

- We will all be responsible for the care of the children in our group and avoid unnecessary interruptions.

- We will keep matters shared in the cell group in strict confidence.

- We will reach out to our family, neighbors, and friends with the goal of bringing at least one person to Christ and to the cell in every six-month period.

Tips

The size of the group cannot grow to more than twelve or fifteen people, or intimacy will be lost. In addition, always sit in a circle, as this allows everyone to have eye contact with each other. The cell leader can then direct the questions to the whole group. People do have a tendency to speak just to the leader. When that happens, the leader should say, "Go ahead and share with the whole group. We all need to hear this."

Exercise love and acceptance, safety and trust. Each person should feel safe about opening up. Each person should be able to trust the cell group with what he says. Be honest with people, try to understand them, and always stress confidentiality. Have fun, but don't get silly; it's not a party. You have to honor the Holy Spirit and the Lord Jesus Christ.

Learn to include silent members or visitors in the conversation by asking questions such as "Have you got something that you would like to share?" or "Would you like to add to that last statement?"

The White Board

Each of the groups should keep an erasable white board on which to write the names of the people for whom you are praying. The names will include lost family members, co-workers and friends, the names of the sick members, and the names of the missionary, zone pastor, and district pastor that the group is praying for. As each prayer is answered, the name is deleted and the group rejoices.

Closing Prayer and Vision

After the discussion period, close the meeting with prayer. Break up into smaller groups of three or four people and pray for each other. If the cell leader tries to pray for the whole group, it will take another hour, and the group will exceed the set time limit. Also, praying in smaller groups is more intense, more personal, more intimate, and more relational. The smaller group should take time to listen carefully to each person's need, then pray specifically concerning that need. Another good rule to follow is that men should pray with men and women with women. There is more openness when the sexes are separated this way. When praying, always encourage people. Never leave them with a heaviness in their hearts or with unresolved, negative feelings.

Powerful intercessory prayer and spiritual warfare should be exercised at the **edification** meetings. At this meeting, pray the roof off. If, however, there are unbelievers present, simply pray *a conversational prayer*. A conversational prayer is one in which we do not speak in tongues and we use simple language as we speak with God.

Testimony of a Cell Leader

The meeting was a blessing. The Lord really moved in the praise and worship and there was freedom. The kids were reverent and open in worship and allowed the Lord to move. The lesson went very well, there was good discussion and many visitors got involved, sharing what was in their hearts. As a result, during ministry we had three young men pray for salvation and four others pray to rededicate their lives to Jesus. Others were blessed and we all were refreshed in the Lord. We are expecting and ready for our vision to be fulfilled. The vision is to reach our town, beginning with our neighbors and friends, and then everyone who crosses our path.

The Vision

Constantly reiterate the importance of what you are doing, and share the vision for your city. Always share the vision of your group as it relates to the greater overall vision of the church. Vision will give the meeting value in the eyes of all who participate. Vision can keep the spiritual fires burning from week to week.

Ministry Opportunities

During and at the end of the meeting, stay sensitive to ministry opportunities within the group. This may be the only chance you get to minister to people. If you notice someone whose heart is breaking, don't just slap him on the back and tell that person you will see him again next week. Pull that person aside and take the time to minister to him. It makes a big difference if you single someone out and show interest in him.

Time Limits

The number one reason people stop going to cell meetings is because the meetings are too long. If we don't have time limits, the meeting will last too long, and long meetings wear people out. The time limit that we've set and found to be most effective is ninety minutes. If we set a ninety-minute time limit and the meeting lasts for an hour and forty-five minutes or two hours, that's okay. If it lasts longer than that, people will stop coming. We must also respect the person in whose home we are meeting. They may need to go to bed early, and they have to clean up after everyone is gone.

There will be times when we'll experience an afterglow because the presence of God is so powerful. If necessary, take the meeting to some other home; God will go also. We must honor the ninety-minute format for those whom we told that the meeting would last only an hour and a half. Let those who desire to do so leave after ninety minutes, and the rest of the people can stay for another twenty or thirty minutes. Do this tactfully by stopping the meeting and announcing that time is up. Stop everything, go to the door, and thank those who are leaving for coming, always inviting them to the next meeting. **Do not make them feel that they are interrupting the meeting.**

+---+
| **Sample Schedule** |
| 15 - 20 minutes ➲ Fellowship |
| 5 - 10 minutes ➲ Planning for next meeting |
| 10 minutes ➲ Worship |
| 10 minutes ➲ Icebreaker |
| 30 - 40 minutes ➲ Discussion |
| 15 - 20 minutes ➲ Prayer and ministry |
+---+

Remember that the Holy Spirit knows what you are trying to accomplish and is not hindered by a schedule. He will move at the appropriate time and accomplish His work.

Chapter 12

Between the Cell Meetings

Ministry that Heals

Marion Slaton had recently moved to Baton Rouge. She had experienced the tragedy of a bitter divorce, the break up of her family, and now on her own, she faced starting life over all alone. However, God knew her dilemma and was about to change her life.

A few days after visiting Bethany World Prayer Center, and having filled out a visitor's card, a knock came on her door. A couple from Bethany, cell leaders, stopped to meet Marion, offered her a decorative loaf of French bread and invited her to a cell-group meeting. At first, Marion was reluctant, but after other visits by the cell leaders, much prayer and several follow-up phone calls, she agreed to come.

Marion spent most of her time, when she wasn't working, sitting at home reading novels and watching television. But this night, the cell leaders came to her house, picked her up, and brought her to the cell meeting. At the cell-group meeting, she began to open up about her situation and the group members gathered around her. One lady in the group reached out and gave Marion a great big hug. That hug changed Marion's life and opened her up to the healing that she desperately needed.

Marion found spiritual life in that group that renewed her faith in God and in people. The group members prayed for her and established a friendship relationship with her. Healing from her hurtful past began that night, and in time, Marion began leadership training. Eventually she became a cell leader, leading a group of her own.

The Cell Group and Beyond

Life and ministry during the cell meeting are very important components for successful cell ministry. If the cell meeting is boring and lifeless, it will soon lose the interest of those involved and fail. Never underestimate the power of an exciting life-filled meeting. But, cell-group ministry does not end with the meeting. There are many other aspects of cell ministry that must be carried out for it to be successful. In this chapter we will look at follow-up, visitation, and building community. We have discovered these three elements at the core of every great cell church in the world.

Three Life-Giving Activities to Do Between the Meetings

- **Prayer**—One activity we have isolated that brings the most results for growth and health in the cell group is prayer. All cell members should develop a prayer life that encircles the people and ministry of their cell group. Praying for others is the lifeline for many folks who, like Marion, need restoration. The cell leader himself should pray daily for members by name and by need. Fasting the day of the meeting until meeting time, coupled with prayer for God's presence and Holy Spirit leadership, is essential for success in the cell group. There must also be an awareness of the enemy's resistance, and the leader and group members should war against this resistance through spiritual warfare and intercessory prayer.

- **Personal contact**—The leader and his intern should contact group members weekly. This can be accomplished by "tele-visits" over the telephone, personal visits at a mealtime, or before and after church services. Sometimes it is appropriate to drop by a person's home or workplace to encourage them or just to chat as a means of staying in touch with them.

- **Follow-up on expressed needs**—Visitors and cell members alike will often express a need at the meeting or during a phone conversation. Always follow up on these needs by telephone, personal visit, or by sending someone else in the group to do so. During a meeting we often make commitments to people to help them or contact them at a later date. We *must* fulfill our commitments to them, carrying out our promises to help.

Look at some of the details of activities between the meetings.

Follow-up

Successful follow-up plans are crucial to building a strong net for new believers and cell members. Many people are lost through the gaping holes in our ministry "nets" and through our large "back doors." Our altar calls have produced scores of souls every week, and God has given us plenty of souls over the years. But where are these people now? After responding for salvation at our altars, being ministered to by a trained counselor, being prayed for and receiving a sincere pat on the back with a "God bless you," these "converts" are often never seen again. From the response at our altars alone, we should experience an increase of many people each year; however, experience has shown that this does not happen automatically. Every local church needs a specific plan for the follow-up and retention of new converts and visitors.

Three categories of people who need follow-up are **visitors**, **converts**, and **cell members**. With the visitors, we want to show appreciation and offer them the right hand of fellowship. With new converts, we want to extend to them our availability and discipleship. With the cell members, we offer relationship. A positive family-like relationship is our goal in all that we do in follow-up.

Visitors

The goal for follow-up on visitors is to meet with them face to face. This is where we get to express an interest in people's lives and offer them fellowship. Often it is an opportunity to verify their salvation, to find out where they stand with Christ. We need to thank them for attending the church service and offer to pray for them. Then, invite them to attend your group and commit to stay in touch with them.

Through "Evangelism Explosion," designed by Dr. James Kennedy of Coral Ridge Presbyterian Church, many churches have experienced great success in taking the opportunity to share the Gospel with people who had visited their church during a recent Sunday service. The cell members can, in the same way, be prepared to share Christ with every visitor who gives them the opportunity.

New Converts

Most recent studies on the subject of follow-up on new converts show that it is imperative for the first phase of follow-up to take place within twenty-four hours of the salvation decision. After that first twenty-four hour period, positive results from follow-up begin to diminish rapidly.

When a person first comes to Christ at the altar, his spirit is open to God in a way that it may never be again. He wants forgiveness for sins that he has committed and help to overcome the problems in his life that have caused him pain and despair. He is ready to exchange his present relationships for new ones which will help bring his life in order, bringing him closer to God. The longer he waits for someone from the church to contact him and have a face-to-face interaction with him, the less open he becomes.

Our experience told us that when we waited a week or two to visit those who had been to our altars, they were no longer open to us, the church, or to Christ. Without the necessary spiritual support of the church, they had already fallen back into their old lifestyles, habits, and relationships. They had committed the sins again that they had repented of two weeks before. They felt embarrassed and disconnected from the very church in which they had so openly and unashamedly walked down to the altar to receive Christ. Now, however, they were feeling guilty and doubting that the feelings that brought them to a place of repentance were ever real.

To prevent this falling away, we put a plan in place for the follow-up of new believers. This plan gives us a face-to-face contact within twenty-four hours with every person who comes to our altars for salvation.

At the altar, the altar worker meets the person and leads that person to the office that cares for the area of the city where the new convert lives. In these offices, cell leaders are waiting for the new convert. After praying with that person and counseling with him, the altar worker collects vital information about the person. Then the worker introduces him to the person who will be responsible for the follow-up of this new convert.

One of the most effective individuals for this follow-up is a member of the pastor's own cell group of twelve leaders he is personally discipling.

This member should be one who is building a new group. This "assimilator" makes face-to-face contact with the new person, introduces himself as the contact person at the church, and exchanges information with him. His first priority is to set up an appointment with the new convert for that evening or at least within 24 hours. This will give the assimilator an opportunity to pray for the needs of that person, see the environment that the person lives in, and meet other members of his family. The pastor may also go on these visits. It is important for groups of two or three to go on these visits, especially when visiting someone of the opposite sex.

The goal during the first visit is to verify the convert's salvation, answer any lingering questions and arrange for that person to be water-baptized. It is essential to be sure that the person responded to the altar call for the specific purpose of receiving Christ as his Lord and Savior.

Armed with all the information that he has obtained from the visit with the new convert, the assimilator continues to make contact with the person by phone, keeping in touch on a regular basis.

The initial contact that the new believer has with the **cell group** can be in his own home with the cell leader. The new believer is brought to the group that weekend, if possible, and there he is assigned a sponsor who will be responsible for ongoing follow-up.

The Encounter Retreat

Bethany World Prayer Center's policy is that every new believer must go through deliverance. It is our experience that The Encounter Retreat or Weekend as it is called, is one of the most important aspects of the cell-church ministry. Without it, we found that most of the new converts would not stay in the church. Why? Because they must go through deliverance from the effects of past sins, life-style, and negative family influences. This is the beginning of the *assimilation* process.

Liver Anyone?

Assimilation works like the liver. The liver is the largest organ in our body and has many different functions. It secretes bile for digestion, metabolizes proteins, carbohydrates and fats, stores vitamins, and removes wastes and toxins from the blood. Basically, it takes the foods that we eat and changes the chemical makeup so that nutrients can be assimilated into the body. Anything that cannot be assimilated is eliminated as waste.

When new believers enter into the Body of Christ through the local church, each one must go through the assimilation process. It is a process of changing the "spiritual chemistry" of each person. This must occur if the person is to become an essential part of the church body. If a person is not rid of the toxic worldly elements, he or she will eventually be rejected by the church. This is a normal and healthy process for the church to go through. Otherwise, people will come into the church with all their addictions and ungodly philosophies of life and will pollute believers.

Conforming the new believer to the image of Christ is the work of the Holy Spirit and the local body of Christian believers. The inability or unwillingness to change on the part of new converts nearly always results in expulsion from the church. They will either be drawn back by their old attachments and connections, or repelled by the members of the church. Think about it. Conversion implies total change. Christ called us to be born again, the most radical picture we can imagine of becoming a new creature. Walking with one foot in the world and the other foot in the church denies our trust in His leading, but without the encouragement of other believers, growth will not usually be as steady. Therefore, the assimilation process is of absolute importance.

The Cell-Group Member

As a cell member now, the new believer receives personal discipleship by the individual assigned to him as his sponsor. The sponsor, who is most often the cell leader, is trained in every step of the discipleship process and is capable of leading this person into a deeper walk with Christ. Through this method of follow-up, a strong bonding occurs between the new convert and his or her sponsor/cell leader. The joy of providing every new convert with this kind of pastoral care is an overwhelming benefit of cell ministry.

Dr. Yonggi Cho, pastor and founder of the Yoido Church in Seoul, Korea, strongly emphasizes visitation to every person in its cell groups. The Yoido Church is reported to have as many as 750,000 members. According to Dr. Karen Hurston, who authored the book *Growing the World's Largest Church*, 600,000 visits are made by the 600-member pastoral staff to the members of Yoido Church every year. One staff pastor commented, "If visitation stopped, I think our church would only be one-tenth its present size."[1]

Breakfast and lunch meetings are very effective times to meet with some working members, but evenings, after work hours, are usually convenient for most.

Cell leaders should make it a priority to make ministry visits with their interns to cell-group members. This is one of the opportunities that they have to equip future leadership in their groups. If possible, the cell leader should spend an hour or more each week with his intern, visiting in homes and hospitals together, sharing times of prayer and planning for the group.

Visitation and Cell Growth

A survey of all our cell groups indicated that groups in which the cell leaders visited their members often and invited cell members to their own homes for social visits had a **much higher growth rate** than cell groups whose leaders did not build these close relationships.

"Tele-visiting" in the evenings (phoning cell members and leaders) is another way to touch the lives of the people in the cell groups. Nothing, however, takes the place of the face-to-face visits. Person-to-person visits are for the purpose of ministry, and many ministry opportunities become available during such visits. The home of a cell member is an ideal place to minister to that person's needs, as well as to the needs of his family.

Guidelines for home visitation were shared with our staff when Dr. Karen Hurston came to consult with us in the first year of cell-group ministry at Bethany. She shared a simple outline for a home visit called the PAM Principle. PAM stands for Pray, Ask, Minister. An example of this principle follows:

When entering a member's home, the first thing a leader wants to do is to set a spiritual tone to the visit. Take a moment to **PRAY** for the person, the family, and the home. The New Testament has several ac-

---

[1] Dr. Karen Hurston, *Growing the World's Largest Church*, Gospel Publishing House, Springfield, Missouri, 1994, p. 114.

counts of Jesus and the disciples entering homes and praying for house-hold members. Prayer prior to the visit is also very helpful in preparing hearts for what the Holy Spirit wants to do through the leader.

After prayer, **ASK** the person to share things that pertain to his life, needs, and desires. To know how to pray, it is important to ask the individual to share. On visits, it is much more important to **listen** than to **talk**! Most people that I visit in the church have waited for an opportunity to speak to me or some other pastor about situations in their lives and to ask questions that have often gone unanswered for months or even years. Give people a chance to say what they want to say. This will provide ample information about them to give you direction for ministry.

Minister

The most productive approach to ministry is to guide the person to the biblical principle or promise that meets his or her need. Have some of the promises of Scripture memorized or written down in a small notebook that can be carried, and read them to the person. Then agree together in prayer that God will meet the needs expressed. It may also be necessary to follow-up on any practical needs that have been expressed. You might want to share with the cell group the practical needs that can be met by the group. The ministry of helps to needy cell members is a great way to express Christian love. Remember, to minister is to serve, and service requires action. Be ready to act on behalf of any cell member who needs help.

Many opportunities for ministry will occur between cell-group meetings. The goal is to care for one another; this caring is called *community*. When a sense of community is present, the cell meeting itself will be enhanced with a new dimension of excitement and expectation. As visitors, new believers, and cell members begin to bond to each other, community will develop, and every life involved will be enriched. Galatians 6:2 says, *"Bear ye one another's burdens, and so fulfil the law of Christ."*

A Closing Thought

Marion Slaton is one of many people who benefited from the follow-up ministry of a cell-group leader. When we become successful in our activities between the cell meetings, we will assimilate more new believers into our local church. These new believers will grow up in Christ in the cell-church ministry and will have an understanding and deep appreciation for all that the cell church provides. They will be motivated to have reproduced in themselves what they saw in the Christians who loved and cared for them.

Chapter 13

Components of the Cell Group

When I walked in the room, I looked around at all the different people, each at his/her own level of maturity and experience. This cell group was not only representative of our church, but of our city. Attendees were of different racial and social backgrounds, and even represented an assortment of denominational affiliations. Each person was at a different level of leadership training with varying degrees of experience to offer in service to the group. Some were there to have specific needs met; others were there just to discover what the group was all about.

The diversity made for an interesting evening. During the meeting I realized how important each human component was to the health of the group. As leader, it was my job to be sure that every need was addressed—whether by me or someone else—and that the life of each individual was enriched.

Within every individual from the group, and within the group collectively, there is the potential to accomplish all that God has planned for them. We must recognize the extraordinary in the ordinary and see potential in people, not simply viewing them as people with potential. There's a subtle difference.

Identifying the Components

Now that I've cautioned you to see the uniqueness of each individual, I'm going to show you the patterns that tend to develop across the board. Although cell groups may vary as to size, construction, and effectiveness, there are certain types of individuals that may be identified in the majority of groups. Below you will find an Illustration of what a "typical" cell group looks like.

If the cell group stops growing and becomes stagnant, it is often because "someone" is missing from the group. In such a situation, the problem can usually be remedied simply by identifying who is missing from the group and formulating a plan to correct the situation.

Leader
Critical **C**are **P**erson
New **M**ember
Children
Growing **M**ember
Visitor (first time)
Intern(s)
Frequent **V**isitor
Mentor (supervising)

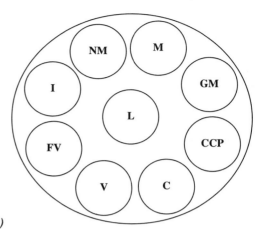

(Figure 13-1)

The list below will prove helpful in pinpointing the problem in a cell group that does not grow.

- No new members—This is evidence of no outreach or assimilation.

- No growing members—This may indicate that no one is on the leadership track, or the group is shallow and non-challenging.

- No interns—If no one is in training, there is no hope of multiplication.

- No mentor—No accountability exists, and the group is characterized by aimlessness.

- No critical care person—The absence of this type of person points to an inward focus in the group.

- No frequent visitors—This may imply a poor quality meeting with no excitement. A lack of prayer may be part of the problem, or meetings may be too long or poorly planned. These are often reasons people don't come back.

- No visitors who are seekers—This may be because of an inward focus, lack of evangelism, no recruiting of visitors, or the group's general lack of interest regarding visitors.

- No children—There may be no children's ministry available in the group, or no one trained to minister to the children. This would keep families with children from attending.

- No leader—This problem exists when a leader burns out and quits because he doesn't know how to manage the group and share responsibilities. It also can happen when there is no one in the group who is in leadership training.

After examining the above list, the pastor or mentor should sit down with the cell leader of a group that is not growing and draw the model of the group in Figure 13-1. The pastor and cell leader should determine together what type of person is missing from the group and then devise a plan to reach out to someone who fits this description. This will help the group to refocus on actually reaching the harvest.

Values of a Cell Group

In addition to having the different types of people present in the group, every cell group must also internalize the dynamic New Testament values that made the church in the book of Acts so successful. Only then can the cell group hope to experience the same powerful results. Look with me at some of the values we have identified that must exist in the local church and its cell groups if true success is to be attained.

Evangelism—There must be a burden for the lost and a sense of responsibility to Christ to fulfill His Great Commission. Praying for and reaching out to the lost should be the heartthrob of every cell group.

Relationships—Building strong bonds between members of the cell group is essential for strong community to become a reality. The goal of every group is to have a community that can care for the needs of each of its members. We need to have an effective community that can replace the old community of the new convert. Otherwise, he will drift back to his previous community and away from Christ.

Transparency—Being open to others in a trusting environment allows people to release inner conflicts and anxiety.

Trust—Because of the desire for openness in each group member, there is a need for confidentiality and safety.

Availability—As needs arise in the lives of those in our group, we need to "be there" for each other. We must learn to readjust our schedules in order to serve others.

Purity—For the testimony of Christ and the group, we need to make sure that we are living pure and honest lives before God and each other.

Awareness—Within the group, we must become sensitive to the needs and concerns of others as well as rejoice with them in the life victories they experience.

Accountability—We must learn to be responsible and answerable to each other for our words and actions, both in and away from the group.

Understanding—It is crucial that we make the effort to understand each other's problems and situations, without being judgmental or critical.

Growth—Knowing that it is God's will for the group to be "fruitful and multiply," we must learn to be willing to release others in the group to pursue their ministry callings and quests for leadership.

Cell-Group Effectiveness

Joel Comiskey has surveyed 900 cell leaders in 8 countries, including 200 in the United States. The results, scientifically analyzed using SPSS, SAS, and Abstat software, provided many new insights. Interestingly, he discovered that the same factors are responsible for the growth of cell groups in every country and culture.[1]

Dr. Comiskey discovered that cell-group leadership that contributes to growth does not depend upon the following characteristics:

• Age

• Gender

• Social, economic, or educational status

---

[1] Joel Comiskey, *Home Cell Group Explosion: How Your Small Group Can Grow and Multiply*, TOUCH Publications, 1998. Lists have been deduced from Summary of Survey Findings on pages 26-28.

- Marital status

- Personality type—Leaders who were types D, I, S, or C were equally effective.

- Spiritual gifting—Groups with leaders with the gifts of service, leadership, evangelism, teaching, etc. grew at the same rate.

However, cell growth was found to correlate clearly with these elements:

- Amount of time the cell leader spent with the Lord each day

- Amount of prayer by the cell leader for cell members—Those who prayed daily for their cell-group members had groups that grew on the average twice as fast as those who only prayed once or twice a week.

- Hospitality, social activity and ministry—The more time cell leaders and members spent together outside the cell meeting, the faster the groups grew.

- Number of visitors—It is not surprising that the more visitors a group had, the faster it grew; but even more important was whether the visitors were contacted by a "follow-up" person.

- Raising up new leaders—Without new leaders, there can no multiplication.

- Clear goals for growth and outreach

- Preparation for the meeting—Poor preparation signals a general disinterest in the group.

The results of this research are very encouraging because they reveal that the factors outside a cell leader's control, such as age, gender, gifting, etc., do not affect the growth of the cell group. All the factors that make a difference are basic principles over which everyone has control and techniques that anyone can put into practice.

The Leadership Track—running the bases

The goal of every cell group is to bring its members through an extensive discipleship process and eventually equip each person to become a leader. The following illustration outlines the steps in that leadership process.

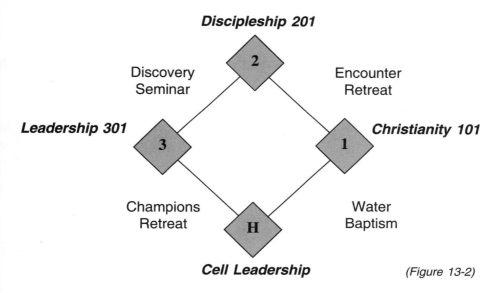

(Figure 13-2)

Remember, the number one reason people stop in their leadership development is that they do not know what the next step is in the process. Below, I briefly explain each step in the process.

- **First Base Path**—Salvation and water baptism—The person accepts Christ and is water-baptized.

- **First Base**—"Christianity 101"—This is a follow-up booklet that assists the cell member in assimilating the new believer into the local church and into the cell group. It is a **six- week process.**

- **Encounter Weekend**—During this six-week period, the person is enrolled in and attends the Encounter Weekend. This is a time to deal with issues of the past in the new Christian's life. Encounter Weekends begin on a Friday evening and continue all day Saturday. During this retreat, each person is introduced to his new life in Christ and is relieved of excess spiritual baggage that he may have brought into his new Christian experience.

- **Second Base**—"Discipleship 201"—This is a twelve-week class that we offer on Wednesday nights or Sunday mornings to help the new believer get grounded in the faith.

- **Discovery Weekend**—At the end of the discipleship classes, the person is encouraged to attend the Discovery Weekend. This is the step in the process where each person takes the D.I.S.C. Personality Profile and the Spiritual Gifts Profile. They come to learn more about themselves as individual personalities, and they also learn what spiritual gifts God has given them.

- **Third Base**—"Leadership 301"—Once a person has completed all the other prerequisites, he can begin attending "Leadership 301." This is a twelve-week class, meeting on Wednesday nights. Once an individual has **started** this class and has submitted an approved leadership application, he may open a group at the pastor's discretion.

- **The Champion's Retreat**—This retreat is a weekend where the new leaders are "ordained" into cell-group ministry. Attending the Champion's Retreat is a statement that they will open a new group within three to six months.

- **Home Base**—When someone opens his own group, he is considered to have reached home plate. This is the destination of every believer at Bethany.

Now, as a leader, you should focus on these three key objectives for a biblical leader outlined on page 38 of Bill Donahue's book *Leading Life-Changing Small Groups*. Bill Donahue is the director of adult education at Willow Creek Community Church in South Barrington, Illinois.

- "Lead through serving your people well."

- "Multiply your ministry into the life of another."

- "Finish the race with integrity."

Minister, Manage, Mentor

For the cell group to grow, mature, and multiply, attention must be given to three specific leadership functions.

- **Minister**—To minister is to serve. Each member of the cell group should learn ministry skills and learn to meet the needs of other members. As needs are expressed in the group, it is the responsibility of **every member** to meet that need. Leaders should encourage the members to get involved in serving as needs are revealed.

- **Manage**—Management of the cell group is often viewed as unimportant because is seems so "unspiritual." The goal of the cell group, however, is to make sure that every member is equipped to eventually lead a group. It is necessary then that the cell leader makes sure that every member goes through the Leadership Base Path and that every member gets the opportunity to lead the cell during his training period. We have noticed that when people do not know what the next step is in the process, they will stop and wait till they are shown. Leaders must constantly recruit members for training classes that are being offered to make sure that they finish the Leadership Base Path and eventually open new groups.

- **Mentor**—As cell members become leaders of their own groups, a deeper relationship between the original leader and his/her member is established. Leaders leading leaders describes this **mentoring relationship.** Before a member becomes a leader of a group, his/her leader ministers to the potential leader and manages his/her training around the Bases. However, when the member opens a group, his/her leader begins to focus on that member's success as a leader. Much more time is spent with the new leader in developing a strong "agape" relationship. This is a face-to-face, heart-to-heart, life-to-life relationship.

Understanding the components of the cell group makes the whole process both exciting and successful. This knowledge will also help you to eliminate the unnecessary and time-consuming parts that bring little or no results. Knowing who should be in the meetings, what is the next step for each in the base path of training, and what activities to focus on, will give the group a greater opportunity for success.

Chapter 14

The Cell-Group Life Cycle

At the ripe old age of 92, Boudreaux passed away in his Cajun town of Pierre Part, Louisiana. The town's mayor and some of the business leaders went to Mrs. Boudreaux to pay their respects. The newspaper editor asked Mrs. Boudreaux, "Mrs. Boudreaux, we want to put somethin' in the obituary column of the newspaper about Boudreaux. What would you like for us to put?"

Mrs. Boudreaux said, "Let me think about dat." Then she replied, "Put in there, 'Boudreaux died!'"

The editor smiled and said, "Mrs. Boudreaux, dat's exactly what happened, but could you think of somethin' more to put in the column?"

Again she replied, "Let me think about dat." Then she said, "Put in there, 'Boudreaux died. Boat for sale.'"

That's right! My mother always used to say when things would go wrong, "That's what you call life." It's true that things don't always go as we wish they would. We are born and we go through many stages in the growing up process. This is also true of cell groups, and any pastor or staff member who is considering cell groups should understand the different stages that cell groups will go through. In his books, *Where Do We Go From Here?* and *The Shepherd's Guidebook*, Dr. Ralph Neighbour speaks of the stages in cell-group life. I've added a couple of stages to clarify the progression, and I liken these stages to courtship and marriage. In order for cells to be successful in a church, the pastor will have to understand how to respond in each stage of the cell group "marriage."

Courtship

When a couple begins courtship, they are learning about each other. They want to make sure they love each other before committing to a life-long marriage. The couple learns all that they can about each other and

154

counts the cost of marriage. The same process should be carried out by the leadership of any local church that is planning to transition into cells. Although there will be obstacles to completing the process, a strong commitment will carry a church to the finish. The Bible says that a man should not begin something that he cannot finish. (See Luke 14:28-30.) The same is true for both marriage and ministry.

On the cell-group level, there should be a time of educating prospective members and a chance for each one to experience cell life before a commitment is made. There is so much that the cell group has to offer, but it may take several weeks for the individual to discover all the benefits.

People are going to have questions when they look at cell groups, the first one being, "Is this for me? Is there a need for this in my life?" This question can be answered only when a person begins to attend a group. Once the group begins, however, the individual will soon discover the dynamics of cell-group life and will want to be a part of it.

The next question often asked relates to the value system of the individual. Often, because of hectic schedules, it is difficult for people to work the meeting into a free time slot in their lives. "Can we live with this ministry in harmony with everything else we are doing?" The answer may be "No." We may not be able to work like we work, play like we play, and spend endless hours in leisure, and still be able to make the time commitment that cell ministry requires. It takes more dedication than just going to church on Sunday and attending an occasional meeting.

Another question that will need to be answered is "Are we willing to sacrifice, prioritize, and change our life values to such a degree that we are able to serve the Kingdom of God in the cell-group ministry?" This is where the "rubber meets the road." If we can say "yes" to that question, we are well on our way into cell-group ministry.

As I commented earlier, marriage is the best way to describe the type of commitment needed for a successful cell church to operate. Once a church is committed and they transition into cells, though members come and go it is difficult to turn back. To achieve this type of commitment, we must first understand the biblical evidence supporting cell groups. *"Day after day, in the temple courts and from house to house, they never stopped teaching and proclaiming the good news that Jesus is the Christ"*

(Acts 5:42 NIV). House-to-house ministry in the Bible is the equivalent of today's cell groups. This type of ministry was so powerful that the Christians of the Early Church turned their world upside down. They evangelized the whole known world in their day.

You will discover the advantages of cell life by actively participating in cell groups. Each person should know what he is getting into before he commits to it. When church members come a few times and start seeing the benefits of cell groups, they will want to participate. If they don't see the benefits of cell groups, then some adjustments in the ministry must be made. If they say, "It was boring," ask what you can do to make the group more interesting. Don't be insulted—change! There have been times in cell ministry that we had to change to meet people's needs and reach souls, but it was worth it! The gospel itself is not a negotiable, but many other items are.

Commitment—the Marriage

After the courtship stage and after the decision has been made that cell-group ministry is for you, you must be ready to make the commitment. You should be able to say, "I want my life to be compatible with this new ministry, and I want the Holy Spirit to be so present in my life that people will be changed through my involvement in this ministry." When we are ready for this change in our lives and families, cell groups are the vehicles that God will use. This was an ever-present element in the New Testament Church.

Some people may say, "I don't think cell-group ministry is God's will for me." Ask them, "What type of ministry is God's will for you?" Encourage them to attend a group and be open to receive something that God is doing in the church. Let them know that through cell-group ministry, they may discover *their* ministry. Based on our experience and the experience of others, eventually testimonies from the cell-group members will be shared more frequently, and it will become obvious that the cell ministry is the way that God is leading the church.

Programs that have been offered in the past will slowly begin to disappear as cell groups replace those ministries. Cell ministry will replace the old home groups, prayer meetings, and other small groups, as well as take the place of many other programs that are in your church now. Cells are not just a temporary solution to church growth problems; cell groups become the lifeblood of the ministry.

The Honeymoon

Now the pastor, pastoral staff, and the congregation are married to cell groups. The next couple of months will be the honeymoon stage. Everyone involved will be excited about having a cell group and experiencing the newness of it all. That is going to keep the flame burning initially. An overwhelming degree of tolerance and grace for anything that happens will also be there. People will simply love the fact that they are a part of what God is doing, and they'll be excited about the possibilities. In this honeymoon stage, there is a sense that nothing can go wrong. It will seem like heavenly bliss. The rapid growth of the cell ministry at Bethany was so exciting during this stage that we seldom saw any problems.

The meetings during this stage should focus on building relationships and exploring each others' worlds. As members get to know each other better, friendships are established and what could be lifelong relationships begin. The honeymoon stage is exciting but temporary. After all, we all know that honeymoons do not last forever.

Conflict Stage

Once the novelty of cell ministry wears off, conflicts may occur. People start becoming comfortable, and they "let their hair down" and begin to speak openly about their feelings and opinions. That's when personalities and values may clash.

When I got married, I thought my wife was perfect. Much to my surprise, as wonderful as she is, she is not perfect. Of course, neither am I. Our imperfections, our flaws, and our lack of character in some areas started surfacing. We could not hide them once we were living with each other every day. Just as in marriage, the cell ministry may at first seem to be the perfect ministry, but imperfections will surface as your church becomes more deeply involved in it. Conflicts will inevitably occur. That's why you have to rely on the power of the Holy Spirit.

When conflicts occur, God will do some maturing in the Church. Proverbs 27:17 says, *"Iron sharpeneth iron; so a man sharpeneth the countenance of his friend."* Thus, when believers are together a good deal, they'll sharpen one another, even if it is through conflict. Through these conflicts, however, relationships are strengthened. During the conflict stage, we must learn how to solve problems. The church that is willing to stick it out and solve problems will last the longest.

Solving Problems

It is imperative that a process for problem solving be in place and followed closely by everyone involved in the work. If there's a problem in a cell group, the leadership should know about it and immediately begin to work closely with the pastors to resolve that problem. If we become expert problem-solvers, we will conquer every threat in our cell ministry.

Community

After the conflict stage, the cell enters the community stage. In the midst of conflict, God is building relationships. Relationships are built in crisis. After a few months, each cell group has become a community. At this point, we start appreciating people, especially people who serve.

In community, we desire to serve more and in better ways. In this stage, something changes and all our struggles begin taking on more meaning. Be assured that through all the conflict, community is being built. So don't despise the conflict; don't despise the struggle. It's only going to make *you* stronger, your *love* stronger, and your *relationships* stronger.

Often I had to work with leaders who were going through conflicts and were ready to quit and give up on God. I loved them and walked with them through their problems. Now when we see each other, there's a totally different look in their eyes, a different respect. We went through that conflict together. We were side by side in the fight, and we made it! We have community with one another.

That's what cell groups are all about—people healing and strengthening and serving others. People will go through hurts and trials, but when it's all said and done, there will be a community. When that camaraderie is developed, we start becoming members of one another, the Body of Christ. Then, all of a sudden, the glory comes, and we see signs and wonders in our everyday lives.

> *But speaking the truth in love, may grow up into him in all things, which is the head, even Christ. From whom the whole body fitly joined together and compacted by that which every joint supplieth, according to the effectual working in the measure of every part, maketh increase of the body unto the edifying of itself in love* (Ephesians 4:15,16).

Outreach and Growth

As these relationships mature, and as the lives of the group members begin to transform into the image of Jesus, conflicts arise. As we go through conflicts, community develops, and our cell group will begin to grow. In the natural or secular world, a good community will experience growth. So, too, when Christians become bonded spiritually, there will be spiritual growth in every area of their lives, and spiritual children will result from that growth.

Evangelism will occur within the structure of the personal community of the individual cell members. As unbelievers come into a meeting that is full of love and meaningful ministry, they will begin to give their hearts to Christ. They will find what those in the lost and problem-filled world have been looking for.

Multiplication

When the group begins to grow successfully and leaders are developed, it is time to multiply into new groups. Through the "Principle of Twelve" (see chapter 17), we help encourage our members to reach out to people with whom they have personal influence to start their own group of twelve. Multiplication should not destroy relationships, but rather facilitate their growth. After all, it is a sign of success, a sign that our goal has been reached. When the group multiplies, leadership multiplies, and new opportunities for evangelism are created with the new cell group.

When we multiply through the "Principle of Twelve," we grow in our commitment to the success of those whom we are mentoring. We maintain the relationships of our group members because they return each week to be mentored. Growth means that we must automatically multiply, and we will. The fruit of evangelism begins to grow and ripen in cell-group ministry. It's a great joy when the harvest is brought in and remains.

Rebirth of the Entire Process

Like farmers, all people love the harvest. When the harvest is ready, they have to get it in, but they can't wait to break up that ground and start all over to raise another harvest. Although the harvest is great, nothing excites them like the possibilities of breaking up the hard ground and getting it ready to receive some new seed.

When a group multiplies, the whole cell process begins all over again. The multiplication of the existing group and the birthing of a new group have been the focus of the cell group from the beginning and now become the focus of the newly formed group.

The entire cycle from new cell group to multiplication usually takes place within six months to a year. This process should never stop happening. It may take longer sometimes, but if we hold to the prayer and evangelistic emphasis of this ministry, we'll see the groups grow. After all, the process of cell ministry involves constant plowing, sowing, and reaping.

Having a Family Party

Make the multiplication meeting like a party. We get the cell-group members together, and we celebrate! The zone or district pastor preaches, and the new leader is honored for starting a new group. There is also safety net in place. The new leaders know that their groups' mentors will be overseeing them in their new position. This encourages them to step out and begin groups of their own, and the entire ministry shares in the joy when multiplication occurs.

Chapter 15

Pitfalls to Avoid

As a Louisiana State Trooper, I had many unusual experiences. This is one of them. While working radar on Highway 190 between Baton Rouge and Opelousas late one night, I clocked a car traveling 95 miles per hour. I thought to myself, "This couldn't be right. No one drives 95 on Highway 190!" I reset the radar unit and sure enough, it clocked the oncoming vehicle at 95 mph. I was on the side of the road about 100 yards past the bridge that crossed the bayou, hidden and out of sight. I turned my headlights on—not my redlights, just the headlights—so when the car passed, I would drive up behind it, turn my redlights on, and pull it over.

I noticed, however, when the car crossed the bayou on the bridge, that it pulled over on the side of the road where I was, thinking that it was another lane of traffic because of my lights. Before I could get out of the way, the car plowed in the back of my patrol car and knocked me about 150 feet down the road and up against a tree. The car that hit me had tumbled over three or four times and landed next to my State Police unit.

I jumped out of my car, put my police hat on, and ran to check on the driver of the speeding car. When I got there, the car was lying on its side. I reached down and pulled the driver up to the window... it was Boudreaux! Boudreaux looked at me with a very strange and astonished expression on his face and said, "Man, you got here fast! This accident just happened!"

Boudreaux has a habit of encountering pitfalls, doesn't he? Whenever we try something new to us, it is certainly helpful to have extra guidance from those who have been there before, so that we can avoid potential problems. The pure cell-church concept in America possesses major advantages that are lacking in conventional program-based ministry: the unique leadership development, the quality of pastoral care provided to the congregation by the groups, and the equipping of church members for ministry are the most obvious ones. Nevertheless, as with any ministry,

there are traps we may fall into that are diversions from the pure cell-church concept and that are eventually fatal to the transition process. The cell church is, at any stage, subject to these pitfalls. We will need to be constantly on guard to avoid these hazards.

The first and most basic concept to grasp is that a church "with" cells is not the same as a cell-based church. Pastor Lawrence Khong of Faith Community Baptist Church in Singapore says, "There is a heaven and earth difference between a church with cells and a cell church."

Here are some of the major pitfalls that must be avoided in order to successfully transition into a cell-based ministry.

Maintaining a Program-based Mentality

The "Power Pill"

While on a trip in Phoenix, my wife and I went to a local laundromat to wash clothes. As we were waiting, I noticed an old "Pac Man" game in the building. To pass the time, I put a quarter into the game machine and began to play. I noticed that "Pac Man" had no problem advancing through the maze and eating up all the squares as long as he got the "power pill." If he failed to get the "power pill," though, he was soon defeated by the "ghosts."

In response to this concept, I have created "Cell Man." "Cell Man" cannot succeed if he does not get the "power pill!" The "power pill" contains human and financial resources, acknowledgment from the pulpit, and the focus of the staff. Cell-based ministry must become the one task that everybody performs together. Let me give you some examples.

Who Gets the Pill?

A very successful pastor of a wonderful church was considering transitioning to cell-based ministry. This church had a very successful Chris-tian education depart-

Cells   **Programs**

ment. It was probably one of the strongest in the city and was staffed with both trained volunteers and a well-educated, paid staff. The problem that existed, however, was that the Christian education department was in **direct competition** with the cell-group ministry. The "top job" in the church was to teach in the Christian education department, not to be a cell-group leader. Therefore, every time someone with ministry potential would vol-unteer, the Christian education department would get that person. The resources, both human and financial, were divided, with the Christian edu-cation department getting the larger share. In other words, Christian edu-cation was getting the "power pill."

As the pastor and I discussed the future of cell-group ministry in his church, I mentioned that he would have to eventually transition the Chris-tian education ministry into cell groups. He had a desire to do just that but knew that it would be unpopular with a major portion of the congregation because of the clout that the Christian education department carried in their church. He had discovered just how difficult it is to have a strong ministry competing with the cell ministry and still have cells be successful.

Temptation to Go Back!

Although we put great emphasis on our Sunday morning celebration services at Bethany, the cell-group ministry gets the "power pill." We use our Sunday services to read testimonies about what God is doing in the cell groups and also to recognize groups when they multiply. Celebration services on Sunday should promote cell ministry and can be very effective in doing so. It is tempting, though, to depend solely on Sunday morning services to be the "launching pad" for cell-based ministry. But, to depend on Sunday services to birth life and ministry in the cell groups takes the emphasis off the ability of the cell groups to do so. Cell groups themselves can produce the life needed for them to self-perpetuate. The Sunday service should embellish the ministry of the cell church, focusing on the general needs of the congregation and helping to unify that congregation in the vision of cell ministry.

There are many good ideas that are program-based in nature that we sometimes want to attach to the cells to help them be successful. **These attachments are simply not needed**. In fact, they will eventually burden the cell groups so much that there will be an overload factor destroying one cell group after another, along with its leadership.

Because of the strength of the cell-church organization, there exists the temptation to use cells to accomplish non-cell tasks. One example is to attach to the cell groups "special needs" ministries that are developed from without the cells. Numerous workbooks and training materials have been developed to reach out to people with addictive behavior, those in broken marriages, single parents, and other individuals with special needs. If we overload our cell leaders with this material and the responsibility to develop these ministries within their groups, we will end up with program-based cell groups. Responsibilities such as these burn out leaders. By their inherent caring and evangelistic nature, however, the cell groups are able to minister to these types of people without adding to the workload of the cell leader.

Special events that are not related to the cell groups can sometimes exhaust the cell leaders and members when done in addition to all the other duties that are required of them in the cell ministry. Some of these events might include such things as evangelistic meetings held in the church, conventions that are not cell related, and social events that require participation by cell members.

The most subtle temptation that hinders the cell-church ministry is the attitude that we must "supplement" what the cell groups are doing with special training seminars and programs in order for them to "really" be successful. This is different from our cell-leader training program, and it sends the very subtle message to the leaders and members that they can't really do the job without the experts coming in and taking over the important responsibilities in certain areas. Actually, the opposite is true. We have found that the cell groups, like cells in the human body, should and can successfully reproduce without exterior support systems. The cells that they reproduce should look like themselves, not like cells that are produced artificially from without the cell.

Once the cell groups are established, we tend to want to revert to our program-based mentality and to begin using the cell groups to carry out our programs. This is devastating to the cells. **Leave them alone!** Let them grow in cell-related ministry. Let them grow in personal discipleship and evangelism skills without loading them down with a lot of extra and unrelated duties.

Other Pitfalls

Whenever an idea is brought up in a staff meeting, or when church members have an idea to start some kind of ministry, ask them and yourself, **"Is this sufficiently related to cell groups?"** Some criteria for determining the relationship of any idea to the cell ministry could be as follows:

- Will this activity **directly** affect the health of the cell groups? How and in what way will it do so?

- What activity is needed that must be carried on outside direct cell group ministry? Is time that is not **"cellular"** in nature being spent in organization and in the use of human resources? Could such activities be carried on at cell-group meetings or as part of normal cell-group activity?

- Does the activity require **focus** and **motivation** from **outside** the cell-group structure? Does the motivation need to come from the pulpit to keep it going? Is the focus on the **method** rather than the people in the groups?

- Does it require leadership that functions **outside** the cell ministry? Does it **compete** for leaders with the cell-group ministry?

- What **direct benefit** does the idea have to cell groups?

Note: To further facilitate the pure cell-church mentality, direct people to the cell groups when they approach you about ministry positions. For example, when people ask you if there is an opening in men's ministry or some other type of ministry, tell them that the cell-group ministry is the direction of the church and that all future ministry will be done in and through cell groups.

There are many other considerations to keep cell-group ministry pure, but these criteria should help us stay in the mainstream of cell-related ministry.

Poor Leadership

Without quality leaders in charge of the management and ministry of the cell groups, the groups will die. Nothing drains the life of a cell group faster than unskilled, unprepared, and misguided leadership. Leaders should develop good facilitation and people skills, an attitude of serving, and an understanding of how to care for the people in their groups. The development of these traits, however, takes time and training. Often the groups will outgrow the leadership base in a local church and put a strain on the cell ministry. At such times, it is better to take the time in training new leaders to begin new groups than to use ill-equipped people as leaders. Have a strong, ongoing, cell-based training process for new leaders to be developed, and don't rush the process.

Aimlessness

Groups must have a defined purpose and direction. If they aim at nothing, they will soon arrive at nothing and perish. Keep the **vision** in front of them!

Evangelism is a key element that keeps the groups focused and meaningful. Without evangelism, the groups become "ingrown" and fall into the **care-group mentality.** A care group can be like the Dead Sea: If there is only input and no output, everything in it will soon die. If the focus of the cell members is just to have their needs met, and they are not concerned about the needs of others around them, they will lose the compassion and sensitivity that are so necessary in giving life to the group.

Evangelism brings growth! It is imperative for cell groups to grow and multiply in order to stay alive. In this aspect also they resemble the cells of the human body. If a group **grows,** it must **multiply.** Multiplication requires the availability of new leaders who have been raised up and trained to assume the leadership of newly formed groups. There should always be a focus on multiplication of the groups. Three ways that groups grow include the following methods:

- Outreach to family and friends by inviting them to the cell-group meetings or to private get-togethers.

- Reaching out to the community by addressing the obvious felt needs of the community. Helping people by cleaning their houses, mowing their grass, fixing their cars, or cleaning a vacant lot in the area are all ways that we have reached out to our community.

- We grow through the assimilation of new converts in our celebration services.

Testimony of Pastor Tony Buchanan, Tullahoma, Tennessee

A year ago we began the transition from programs to cells with 5 cells and 33 participants. Our church attendance was in the 50 to 60 range on Sunday mornings.

Today we have 7 cells with approximately 70 participants. Since the beginning of the year, 47 people have joined our church and attendance on Sundays has about doubled. Between our outreach team and the cell evangelism events we have seen approximately 64 confessions of faith and a number of re-dedications. Most exciting has been to see our people catch the need for personal evangelism. Cells are starting to turn us around and make us the church we always thought the Lord wanted us to be.

Selfishness

The question "What's in it for me?" demonstrates the typical American mentality. Unfortunately, we have been trained to expect something in return for anything we do. The fear of sacrifice has kept us from many of the true blessings of God. Many people will come for what they can "get out of the meeting," instead of for what they can contribute. True spiritual growth and community, however, come from sacrifice; therefore, keep the groups focused on their **service** to the Kingdom of God and the community around them. The goal of every group is to bring each person from the receiving mode into the giving mode, helping each person to become a contributor in the group and in life.

Ignoring Relationships

Although having an efficient structure is good and necessary, having relationships is even better! For the purpose of assimilation of new believers, we have divided our city and surrounding area into **districts** and **zones**. We have pastors assigned to each area, and we ask them to spend their time developing that area. We group the cells by zip codes to form these districts and zones; however, we emphasize relationships, through the Principle of Twelve, as the major criteria for cell-group ministry. If we force people to attend by zip code groupings only, they will eventually quit coming. People want to go to a group where they *know others,* even if it is across town! As groups grow and multiply, they become more relational. Because of the principle of twelve, relationships are the basis for most cell growth and multiplication. We use geographical boundaries primarily for the purpose of assimilation.

Giving Homework

As pastors, we want to make sure that every soul in our church is trained in the Word of God and in practical Christian living. It is unreasonable to think, however, that they have plenty of time to spend at home studying lessons that they get from the cell group each week. Insist that all assignments must be completed before they return to the next meeting, and no one will show up!

One of our pastors took over the leadership of a group that I had led. It was comprised of missionary families who had returned from the mission field. The pastor was a very capable leader, and the cell members were very mature individuals. He gave us all a homework assignment that probed some of our feelings and asked for detailed answers. Only one couple showed up at the next meeting... it wasn't me and my wife!

Frivolous Discussion Topics

People are starved for the **"real meat"** of Christianity! They often deal with surface issues all day long or with job-related matters that are routine and monotonous. Give them real food from God's Word. Don't let the cell members perish because of spiritual malnutrition. They need to be engaged in discussion topics that challenge their minds and souls. They also need spiritual interaction with other Christians where they can participate in both **body ministry** and **exciting interaction with the Holy Spirit.** This will keep them coming back for more!

Lack of Flexibility

Strictly controlled schedules that allow meetings to be held only on a certain evening of the week can restrict some people from coming. Don't limit access to the groups! Be sure that you are not in competition with work schedules, church activities or services, or other events that compete "head-on" with cell-group meetings. We can expect, however, for people to be willing to adjust certain aspects of their schedules in order to participate. We can't adjust to every member's schedule, but we should be aware of obvious conflicts.

Lack of Structure

Two major factors that have helped our groups to be successful are **careful planning** and adherence to a **successful format**. It is refreshing when the Holy Spirit moves in a group in ways that we didn't anticipate, but total spontaneity in every meeting can keep people away. People will quit coming to cell groups if the meetings are too long, or if the meetings are too unpredictable.

If a person attends a group whose meetings last between ninety minutes and two hours and provides both childcare and in-depth ministry for himself, he'll continue to participate. However, if he is not sure how long the meeting will last or conversely, if he knows that it will likely last into the early hours of the morning, or if he is not sure that anyone has even thought about childcare, he'll probably stay home. Don't confuse *spontaneity* with spirituality. The Holy Spirit is the most organized Person in the universe, and we should learn some management skills from Him! We believe that the Holy Spirit has given us the wisdom for the structure of our meetings, a structure that gives Him greater opportunity to accomplish His purposes in the groups.

People enjoy **well-planned meetings** in which they feel some **ownership**. Let the group plan the next week's meeting each week before they are dismissed. Input from everyone will benefit the ministry of the cell group.

Money Matters

In some countries and even in some churches in the United States, offerings and tithes are taken up in the home at the cell-group meeting. If this is to be done in cell groups, make sure that it is well supervised and managed. When tithes and offerings are normally collected at the main church services, there is no need to take them in the cell group.

If the policy is to take up offerings in the cell groups, be aware of some potential dangers. There are situations when a group wants to take an offering for another member or someone else they know who has expressed a need. This should be done only with the approval of the zone or district pastor. Too often, however, we discover people with their "hand out" who are not in dire need or are "professional" beggars. They learn how to make their way through the entire cell-group system, getting money from different groups. Always keep a record of any money that is collected at a meeting, and note the purpose for which it was taken. A minimum of three trusted people should verify all offerings. This helps minimize fraud.

Business in the Cell Group

Because of its structure, the cell-group ministry can be a target for people who want to take advantage of its organization for personal business reasons. One of the major culprits is the multi-level marketing type of business. Although nothing is wrong with working for a multi-level business, using the cell group for obtaining contacts is forbidden.

Investment opportunities are another scam that can destroy cell groups and their members. There are many horror stories of people being taken advantage of after having developed a trusting relationship with someone who wanted them to get involved in a business or investment scheme.

Any investments that a cell member makes should be handled by trust-worthy, licensed investment agents, not by friends in his cell group. The leadership of the church should constantly remind members about the dangers of involvement with people in business through cell-group contacts.

Borrowing money from other cell members should also be discouraged. This can cause hurt and distrust among all parties involved. A good example of this would be the time a man asked one of the ladies in the cell group to loan him a substantial amount of money. She didn't have the cash, so she borrowed money for him against her credit card. He never paid her back. Don't loan money in the cell group!

These are normal pitfalls that affect any church or church structure. Because of the vulnerability of the cell groups, however, there is a need for greater supervision and interaction with all cell group members to ensure that money-related pitfalls are avoided.

Handling Problem Situations

When handling problem situations, we need to use all the wisdom that God has given us. The Scriptures admonish us to be as *"wise as serpents, and harmless as doves"* (Matthew 10:16b). Without warning, certain individuals can disrupt a cell-group meeting and destroy the atmosphere of unity and ministry. The leadership in the cell group should move quickly to identify, get under control, and minister to any disruptive or potentially problematic person. Do not ignore problematic people, but deal with them in a firm but loving spirit. Galatians 6:1 states, *"Brethren, if a man be overtaken in a fault, ye which are spiritual, restore such an one in the spirit of meekness; considering thyself, lest thou also be tempted."*

Our goal in such situations is restoration of the person and ministry to his needs. There may be a time that discipline or even expulsion from a group is needed; if so, that should be left up to the pastoral staff.

We also want to protect the members of the group from the harm that disruptive people can sometimes cause. The following chart gives some basic insights to problems that can occur in a cell group and how to handle each given situation.

CHARACTERISTICS	DANGER TO GROUP	HOW TO HANDLE
Super-spiritual 1. Seeks domination 2. Seeks attention 3. Critical of leaders 4. Tries to impress members, egotistical	**Disunity** 1. Deceives the younger Christians 2. Disrupts the flow of the meeting and the ministry of the Holy Spirit 3. Tries to get "followers"	**Firm Leadership** 1. Do not allow the person to dominate the conversation. 2. Stay on the discussion topic. 3. Deal with all disruptions during and after the meeting firmly and with love
Someone Else's Disciple 1. Shares the vision and information from another group or person that's outside the local church 2. Openly disagrees with our doctrine or ministry style 3. Not submitted to the leadership of the group	**Disillusionment** 1. Causes confusion about the purpose of the group 2. Causes strife over doctrine 3. Can divide the group and discourage new believers	**Firm Correction** 1. Personally take person aside and clarify the purpose of the cell group. 2. Tell the person that he can attend, but will not be allowed to sow discord. 3. Do not encourage his disruptive sharing.
Self-appointed Pastor 1. Has a possessive spirit 2. Criticizes church leaders 3. Recruits followers to himself 4. Roams from group to group, looking for recognition	**Diversionary** 1. Leads members away from the group 2. Steals sheep from the local church 3. Diverts attention from church leaders onto self	**Limit Access** 1. This person should not be allowed to attend if he diverts members away from the group or church. 2. Require that he be submissive to the leadership of the group and local church.
Blabberer/Rambler 1. Carries on a one-sided conversation 2. Shares stories that are irrelevant to the subject being discussed 3. Dominates the discussion time	**Frustration** 1. This person causes "dead space" during the meeting. 2. The meeting becomes boring and one-sided. 3. There is a loss of spiritual energy in the group.	**Limit Sharing** 1. Make the person aware of his tendencies. 2. Do not encourage or call on him to share. 3. Set time restraints on his sharing.

CHARACTERISTICS	DANGER TO GROUP	HOW TO HANDLE
"Senior" Christians 1. Long time member of the church and is not interested in the group as much as in his own experiences 2. Has a superior attitude and "position" because of his long-time membership in the church 3. Lives in the past	**Intimidation** 1. Younger Christians are intimidated by his experience. 2. Comments on how it "used to be" sow discontentment in the group. 3. This person may display a non-submissive attitude that breeds rebellion.	**Teach Equality** 1. Exhibit equality in dealing with this member. 2. Don't allow the idea of seniority to gain position. 3. Treat every member with the same level of respect.
Critic/Complainer 1. Never satisfied with the meeting 2. Critical of everything in the group and church 3. Self-centered 4. Negative attitude	**Negativity** 1. His negative attitude discourages group members. 2. His self-centeredness draws the focus off the purpose of the group.	**Stop Immediately** 1. Critical attitudes and complaining will undermine the purpose of the group and kill it. 2. Stop him! Insist that he refrain from talking.
Incorrigible Person 1. Unable to reform or be corrected 2. Resists all authority 3. Refuses to cooperate with leader of group 4. Becomes actively disruptive	**Disruptive and Divisive** 1. This person sows rebellion and confusion. 2. He destroys the unity of the group. 3. He discourages participation of the other members.	**Strong Leadership** 1. Now is the time to exert strong leadership. 2. Stop immediately! 3. Protect the group from the person's influence. 4. Refer him to the zone or district pastor.

The goal is to keep the group healthy and growing. One of the best ways to do this is by always letting pastors know how the group is going and informing them of any potential problems. Good communication is essential at every level.

Chapter 16

Mentoring

One day, after several weeks of feeling puny, Boudreaux went to the doctor's office. When he walked in for his appointment, the doctor noticed that Boudreaux had a banana in one ear, a carrot in the other, and a crawfish in his nose. Boudreaux looked at the doctor and said, "Doc, I don't feel good!"

The doctor said to him, "Don't worry about dat none, Boudreaux. We gonna get to the bottom of dat. I done bought me some high-tech medical machines, and after I run some tests on you, we gonna know what's da matter with you. However," the doctor added, "I can tell you something right now, Boudreaux. You ain't eating right!"

Mentoring Leadership

If all problems were as obvious as that facing Boudreaux, we probably would only need some occasional advice. The fact is, though, many of the spiritual obstacles we'll encounter will be subtle ones. If we are to experience steady growth in our Christian walk, the faithful friendship of someone who is farther along in Christ will be a blessing of tremendous value.

Immediately after becoming a Christian, I was introduced to A.E. Eccles, a pastor who had planted over a dozen churches in the Baton Rouge, Louisiana area and was respected by the scores of pastors who knew him. Of all the Christian men that I met and knew as a young Christian, Brother Eccles, as we called him, was the main one who really took an interest in me. I was a state policeman at that time but had a real hunger for the Word of God. Brother Eccles knew that, and without my realizing the significance of what he was doing, he took me under his wing; that is, he became my mentor.

For many years Brother Eccles taught me the Word of God, gave me insights on how to walk the Christian faith, and, most importantly, taught me how to minister to others. Like no other person I knew, he demonstrated humility, devotion to the Bible, and holiness. He continually answered my unending questions with exceptional patience. He was a true "discipler" of men. Over the years I have met many others whom Brother Eccles mentored, and they too revere the man for pouring his life into them.

On the contrary, however, there are men in my own cell group who have never had anyone to speak into their lives, especially when they were children. One man in my group expressed that the one and only thing that he remembered his stepfather teaching him was "Finish what you start." That principle has stayed with him for all these years. Imagine what that man might have gained if his stepfather had intentionally mentored him during his childhood years!

In 1975, while still a state policeman, I was leading a small prayer and Bible study group in my home outside of Chatham, Louisiana, in an area known as "Hoghair, Louisiana." On several occasions Brother Eccles drove the nearly four-hour journey to my home in this remote area simply to teach the group. While on a visit one day, he looked at me and said, "Brother Hornsby, you are a pastor." I argued for a moment with him, contending that I was only trying to help people to know Christ better. Within one year, however, I found myself starting Victory Fellowship, a new local church in West Monroe. It was on the strength of Brother Eccles' words and by the confirmation of the Holy Spirit that I realized my calling. What I gained from him over the ensuing years was not taught to me in seminary, neither did I learn it from books—it was the direct result of the mentoring process.

As a natural response to being mentored for so many years by Brother Eccles, I began to do the same for many others in my church in West Monroe. Over the seven-year period that I was pastor of that church and in the time immediately following, eight men and women were placed on the mission field. As of this writing, many are still serving in missions or are pastors of local churches.

Three Benefits of Being Mentored

- **Relationship**—The first and most important benefit of being mentored is having an intimate relationship with someone who can help you grow. In Brother Eccles, I had a man in my life who was more knowledgeable, more experienced, and wiser than I. My relationship with him caused me to grow in knowledge and maturity as a young Christian and pastor. I had a connection with Brother Eccles that made me feel comfortable when approaching him, and I possessed the security of knowing that I had someone to go to when I needed help.

- **Direction**—The second benefit of being mentored is having someone in your life to give you direction. Through the many phone calls and face-to-face conversations that I had with my mentor, I was constantly able to receive the necessary direction for any stage in my spiritual life or ministry; consequently, I never felt alone and aimless. The timely words of Brother Eccles not only kept me from making major mistakes, but also stopped me from following every wind of doctrine.

In his book, *Mentoring*, Bob Biehl defines the mentoring relationship within the scope of two questions that the mentor should ask the protégé: **"What are your priorities?"** and **"How can I help you?"** Priorities can be goals or problems. They may be personal or professional. Once we have established the priorities, we have a clearer picture of what the job will entail. As a mentor, you may need to help your protégé decide upon a course of action, or you may simply provide resources to help him achieve his goals.

The direction that was given to me by my mentor was often a timing issue concerning what step to take *next* as I led the group that I was teaching. One of the greatest hindrances to the ability of new believers to become leaders is *not knowing the next step* in the process. People will wait indefinitely for someone to show them what should be done next. The mentoring process involves a sensitivity in giving direction on an incremental basis. For each step along the way, there should be a clearly marked path. Your mentor can help you discover your spiritual calling and teach you all the skills necessary to be effective in that calling. The leader/disciple relationship can not be gained merely by attending Sunday and Wednesday night services. Rather, leadership qualities are most effectively transmitted in a *mentoring relationship* where on-the-job experience is gained.

- **Role Model**—Nothing takes the place of being able to watch and learn from a mature Christian who is experienced in ministry. I learned to pray by observing my mentor pray, how to preach by observing him preach, and how to study the Bible by following his example of love and respect for the Word of God. How else can we learn these important values unless we see them demonstrated before our eyes? Just as Jesus led his disciples by example, so, too, does the mentor lead by the actions he performs before those he influences.

An unforgettable moment that I experienced with Brother Eccles occurred the day my wife and I were waiting for him to arrive for a luncheon date. He was driving up from south Louisiana to our home in the northern part of the state, but when he didn't show up and was over three hours late, we became concerned that something might have happened to him. As I drove down the gravel road that led from my house to the highway, I noticed a car pulled to the side of the road, and there was Brother Eccles, leaning over a fence post reading his Bible! I stopped my car and walked over to Brother Eccles, getting his attention. I remarked that we had worried about him and reminded him of the lunch appointment. He apologized and admitted that he had paused to finish reading a portion of his Bible. Then he said to me, "Brother Hornsby, I'm reading Romans, and I'll tell you, **this is rich**!" His example gave me such a love for the book of Romans that during my first pastorate I taught Romans nearly continuously for seven years.

Recently, my middle daughter, Trudy, was visiting me, and I saw on the bookshelf the Bible I had used during "the Brother Eccles era." I asked her to pick it up, look at its side, and open it to where she saw the most space between the pages. She opened it right to the book of Romans! I remarked, "Do you know why it opens to Romans?" She shook her head. **"Because Romans is rich**!" I answered.

Mentoring—The Key to Lifelong Productivity

Isaiah 8:16, *"Bind up the testimony, seal the law among my disciples."*

Matthew 8:23, *"And when He was entered into a ship, his disciples followed him."*

John 3:25, *"Then there arose a question between [some] of John's disciples and the Jews about purifying."*

In the above Scriptures we see biblical evidence of the mentoring process of both Old Testament and New Testament leaders. In these examples we are exposed to a means of teaching and training people that is not common in our society today. In many of our training institutions, scriptural and historical truth is often excluded because there is a liberal, unbelieving teacher or professor at the helm. Becoming more prevalent is the omission of facts concerning the godly heritage of our society or the rewriting of historical events in a critically biased fashion in our children's textbooks. These facts make mentoring a crucial issue in the church today. To ensure that truth is passed down from one generation to another, godly men and women must engage their children and peers in a mentoring relationship.

Testimony of Pastor Ted Long from Bethany World Prayer Center

In my cell meeting last week, one of our discussion questions was "Who was most significant in your life in helping to disciple you in the way of the Lord, and how did they do it?" The discussion that followed didn't seem to be answering the question, so I re-phrased the question and asked, "How many of you were discipled or mentored by someone in your Christian walk?" To my surprise, no one raised his or her hand. I followed up with another question, "How many of you are discipling or mentoring someone other than your children?" Again, no one raised his or her hand. They began to tell why they weren't discipling others. People were too busy, and they weren't interested in a discipleship level of commitment.

Intrigued by their responses, I asked a third question, "How many of you have wanted someone to disciple or mentor you?" To my surprise, every hand went up.

It occurred to me that we all know something about parenting because we have all had parents—whether they were good or bad, single or married, adoptive or foster parents. We all learned something about parenting that gives us a starting point. However, if we have never been discipled by someone, we may not have much more than a clue how to go about discipling someone else.

We are being called to return to a New Testament model of ministry, where we make disciples rather than converts. The Early

Church was so involved in each other's lives and committed to each other and the Lord that they were willing to sell their goods and have all things in common. Perhaps, there has to be a generation that is willing to re-start the discipling/mentoring process so the next generation will have it so ingrained in them that they will be natural disciple-makers.

Becoming a Mentor

What is a mentor? "A wise and faithful advisor or tutor," according to *The Living Webster Encyclopedic Dictionary*. In my experience, a mentor is also a role model, someone who provides a valuable system for passing down specialized and critical information and experience. The protégé is someone to whom the mentor is connected and who will carry on the mentor's vision.

"Many a man would rather you heard his story than granted his request." — Phillip Stanhope, Earl of Chesterfield.

What Will I Do As a Mentor?

- **Add value to others**

If you strive to add value to people, they will let you mentor them. You must live your life for the benefit of those you mentor—family, friend, protégé. How is this done? Look at the performance principles from Zig Ziglar.[1]

1. *"Look for the good in others."*

2. *"Remember that action often precedes the feeling."*

3. *"Catch them doing something right."*

4. *"Seize the opportunity to share a sincere compliment."*

5. *"Praise in public, censure in private."*

---

[1] *Top Performance*, published by Berkley Books, New York, New York, 1986, p. 66.

- **Lift others up**

  You must strive to bring people to a higher level of life and productivity. However, you must allow them to live on the level that they determine is best for them. You cannot force a higher life on them, only encourage it.

- **Reproduce the mentoring concept**

  Ask the protégé if he is willing to reproduce other mentor/leaders if you invest in developing him. This perpetuates the mentoring culture. It is difficult to mentor if you have never been mentored. The benefit of establishing a chain of discipleship is described in the Bible. *"And the things that thou hast heard of me among many witnesses, the same* **commit thou to faithful men**, *who shall be able to* **teach others also"** (II Timothy 2:2, emphasis added).

- **Reproduce Christ in others**

  Mentoring is the influence that you have in a person's life; it is not a position over your protege. We teach people what we know; **we reproduce what we are**.

- **Recruit others for the vision**

  You begin the relationship by asking people to become part of a great vision. Having a cause worth dying for is the greatest reason to live. You don't mentor others just to have followers, but to have them involved in that great vision.

Whom Do I Mentor?

- People with whom you already have influence. People who look up to you for counsel and wisdom.

- People who have potential.

- People who want you to be their mentor.

- People who need a mentor/father.

- Friends of those you mentor who would benefit from the relationship and from your wisdom.

Five Levels of Mentoring [2]

- **Status** — "I have the right to be followed and to speak into your life, because I am **over** you."

  Your influence in a person's life because of status or position will not extend beyond the lines of the place where you hold status. Most people think this is the pinnacle of influence. It becomes a control issue instead of a personal interest issue. The fabric of this relationship is built on **title** instead of respect.

  People will not follow a <u>positional</u> relationship past their stated authority.

  In any event, Baby Boomers are unimpressed with status or symbols of authority.

- **Friendship** — People follow because they know you and like you.

  In this level people will follow you even when they are not required to.

  Friends want to be around you because you care for them.

  On this level, time, energy, and focus are placed on the individual's needs and desires.

  If you cannot build solid, long-lasting relationships, you will not mentor a person for any length of time. The mentoring lasts only as long as the relationship.

- **Productivity** — People follow you because of what you have helped them to accomplish.

  On this level, needs are met and the people you mentor become more successful, feel more secure, and gain confidence in themselves be-

---

[2] Deduced from John Maxwell's "Leadership Is Influence" Seminar in Alexandria, Louisiana, October 27 and 28, 1997.

cause of their personal achievements.

On the productivity level, people get together to accomplish a purpose and to go to a higher plain of success.

They enjoy the results-oriented nature of the relationship. Mentoring and ministry occur for a higher purpose than just fellowship.

If a person does not learn to accomplish his goals, he may never be fulfilled. The relationship that the mentor has with his protégé can bring the person to a high level of productivity.

- **Replication** — In time you will begin to reproduce yourself in others.

When you begin to empower others with your wisdom and encouragement, they will begin to become successful in their lives. Your direct influence on their lives enables you to reproduce in them the qualities that you have in your life.

Your goal is to produce a "successor." Success without a successor is failure.

The people that you surround yourself with in this mentoring process will be people that you have personally touched or helped to develop in some way.

Systematically meet with and share heart-felt issues with those whom you mentor. They, in turn, will pass on to others what you have given to them.

- **Honor** — Over time people will honor you for your contribution in their lives.

After years of pouring your life into people, they will begin to understand the value of your mentoring them. With that comes honor.

Every thought of you and the time you spent with the people you mentored will be remembered for the difference it made in their lives.

Your example of mentoring will be emulated by those you influenced.

The greatest honor of all is to have your life reproduced in others and by others.

Five Reasons We Mentor[3]

- **Nurture Maturity**—Young men and women need to be guided into adulthood. The mentoring process fosters mature thinking and actions, and cultivates responsibility and confidence during the developing years.

- **Stabilize Society**—With society changing so rapidly, especially in the realm of technology, it often appears that the values of the "technical genius" have more merit to our young people than the values of our moral leaders. Mentors help keep the moral standards relevant to our youth and potential leaders.

- **Reach the Displaced**—We live in a mobile society where many children grow up in areas where they have no relatives. They lose the influence of their uncles and aunts, grandparents, and close family friends. The mentor helps provide the oversight and input not available through absent family members.

- **Shrinking Status**—There are not many Christian leaders around who are a voice for absolutes, values, and principled living. If we don't provide a mentoring base for our generation, our values could be lost. In 2 Kings 22, we read the story of Josiah rediscovering the Law with its values and principles. Israel had existed for decades under evil kings and had suffered greatly because of the loss of biblical values.

- **Preservation of Heritage**—Many of the textbooks in our nation have totally omitted the facts that relate to the forming of our nation by godly men and women. There is an intentional avoidance of any reference to the Judeo-Christian ethic that we as a Christian community embrace. Who will teach our children these ethics? It is the role of the mentor to pass this information to the next generation.

---

[3] Concepts drawn from *Mentoring* by Bob Biehl, Broadman and Holman, Nashville, TN, 1996, pp. 11-13.

List five people that you want to start a mentor/protégé relationship with.

1. _____

2. _____

3. _____

4. _____

5. _____

Mentors in Scripture

Providing guidance, passing down timely and critical information, and life-to-life transmission of God-given resources partially describe what mentoring is all about. In the next paragraphs we will look at how the Apostle Paul influenced Timothy's life.

The book of Second Timothy holds the secrets of Paul's life as a mentor. His relationship with Timothy and the instruction that he gives Timothy reveal Paul's heart as a "father in the faith."

Three things stand out in this relationship:

1. **Love**—*"To Timothy, my dearly beloved son"* (II Timothy 1:2). The greatest quality of a mentor is his ability to love his protégé. In a sermon preached at our church, Pastor Larry Stockstill brought out three aspects of love that I feel are critical in expressing the "agapé" love of God.

   • **Sacrifice**—"I live for you." Living for someone else's success and happiness is an irrevocable condition of being a mentor.

   • **Sensitivity**—"I listen to you." So many people in ministry are so focused on their own success, they never get around to listening to the dreams of others in the church who look up to them and need their affirmation.

• **Surrender**—"I learn about you." Understanding that we are different from each other and being willing to discover *why*, goes a long way in encouraging the mentor/protégé relationship.

2. **Prayer and support**—*"without ceasing I have remembrance of thee in my prayers night and day"* (II Timothy 1:3b). Specifically pray for the following areas:

• Their ministry to others (II Timothy 4:2-4)

• Their endurance in affliction (II Timothy 2:3)

• Their faith and walk in Christ (II Timothy 3:14-17)

• Their purity and sanctification (II Timothy 2:19-26)

• Their multiplication of disciples (II Timothy 2:2)

3. **Have constant contact with your protégé**—*"Greatly desiring to see thee, being mindful of thy tears, that I may be filled with joy"* (II Timothy 1:4)

• To impart spiritual gifts (II Timothy 1:6, Romans 1:11)

• To impart truth and sound words (II Timothy 1:13)

• Impart values (II Timothy 3:10-14)

• Fellowship (II Timothy 4:9,21)

Mentors as Fathers

*As it is written, I have made thee (Abraham) a father of many nations, before him whom he believed, [even] God, who quickeneth the dead, and calleth those things which be not as though they were. Who against hope believed in hope, that he might become **the father** of many nations, according to that which was spoken, So shall thy seed be* (Romans 4:17-18, emphasis added).

There has never in the history of our nation been a time such as this where fatherhood has been so grossly neglected. The obvious problems that face this nation begin in the home and with the fathers. Consider the following points.

The Absence of Fathers

In today's society there are many "Timothys" looking for Pauls, but very few Pauls willing to take on the responsibility for the Timothys. These local statistics for the parish (county) in which I live give us some insight into the problem.

—75% of the public school students are not in a traditional family environment. This is a result of absent fathers.

—Children want models and mentors more than programs and systems. When asked, "What are the main problems in the school system?" the children answered, "Sex, drugs and violence."

—Hopelessness is the prevailing emotion in our society because there are no fathers at the family level to lead and guide the children. Fathers should be the "hope-givers" in the family by providing food, shelter, encouragement, and education to their children.

Mentor/protégé relationships were **developmental relationships**. The most commonly posed question to the student was not, "What are you studying?" but rather, "Who are you studying under?" You were known as your mentor's disciple, e.g., the disciples of John, Jesus' disciples, or in the Old Testament, sons of the prophets, or the sons of whatever tribe you belonged to. This indicated to the one asking what your thoughts, philosophy, and standards of conduct were, or more importantly, who your mentor was. Fathers fulfill the developmental role in their children's lives.

These biblical relationships were established to "stimulate" and to "encourage" each other. *"And let us consider one another to provoke unto love and to good works: Not forsaking the assembling of ourselves together, as the manner of some [is]; but exhorting [one another]: and so much the more, as ye see the day approaching"* (Hebrews 10:24-25).

A Father Is a Developer of His Children

Jesus constantly confronted the Pharisees, who saw themselves as the "Fathers of Israel." They may have been the rulers in the positional sense, yet for all their claims to the title, they did nothing to live out the true role of fatherhood. Fathers live to serve the interest of those that they lead; this was not the case of most Pharisees.

The term "father" relates to the person whose way of life and faith reproduces the same in others. The father becomes the central figure in his children's (or protégé's) life as he cultivates character, godly habits, and ethics in them. He also acts as a counselor and trainer to bring his children to adulthood and productivity. It is life-to-life transmission of truth and skill.

How does the father's role compare to that of the teacher, coach, or boss? Each of these people are important to our lives for obvious reasons. Some can have a negative impact on our lives as well as a positive impact. Each is an authority figure with differing degrees of value to us. As we compare the level of importance below, we assume that the impact of each person is for positive results. When the responsibility for mentoring those under our oversight is neglected, it can leave a gap of learning and maturity in their lives. We must realize that God has put mentors here to build lives.

We see the difference in these titles as we compare them.

	Father	**Teacher**	**Coach**	**Boss**
Duration:	Lifelong	School years	Athletic years	Time on job
Acquires:	Sires	Assigned	Selects	Hires
Responsibility:	Gives life	Gives lessons	Gives training	Gives a job
Committed to:	Well-being	The subject	The game	The work
Provides:	Home	Classroom	Playing field	Workplace
Life Benefit:	Leaves an Inheritance	Education	Sense of Team	Paycheck
Permanent Results:	Heritage	Diploma	Trophy	Retirement

Every person is important in our life, but not all are fathers. I Corinthians 4: 14–16 states, *" I write not these things to shame you, but as my beloved sons I warn [you]. For though ye have ten thousand instructors in Christ, yet [have ye] not many fathers: for in Christ Jesus I have begotten you through the gospel. Wherefore I beseech you, be ye followers of me."*

The Mentor as a Father Figure

- He is a **discipler**—helping with the basics of following Christ.

- He is a **spiritual guide**—providing accountability, direction, and insight for maturity

- He is a **coach**—giving motivation and skills needed to meet the challenge

- He is a **counselor**—sharing timely advice, perspective on self, others, and ministry

- He is a **teacher**—conveying knowledge/understanding of the subject at hand

- He is a **sponsor**—providing career guidance, protection, relational networking.

- He is a **model**—exemplifying a living, personal example for life, ministry, career, and family[4]

Mentors Make Dreams Come True

John Proodian moved to Zachary, Louisiana to become a member of our church because he was convinced that the cell-church structure was what he needed in his life. He quickly embraced the mentoring concepts that we taught and began to put them into action. John owns a small computer business.

On several occasions, John has taken young men under his wing to

---

[4] Material adapted from page 6 of *The Greatest Mentor in the Bible* by Tim Elmore, Kingdom Publishing House, Denver, CO, 1996.

mentor them in computer-related work. His goal is to help these men improve their skills until they know enough to break into one of the computer fields that they have an interest in. This is a very important concept.

David Bezet, my son-in-law, has been in the management circles of a construction supply company for many years. He has had a desire, however, to improve his situation where he could realize his full potential in life. His interest is in the computer field, but after working 50-60 hours per week, he has very little time and energy left to study sufficiently to make the transition.

David met John Proodian during the time this book was being written. John has agreed to work with David and mentor him until he is able to get a job in the computer industry. God is using John in a very practical way to help David realize his dream and is opening up to David a whole new way of life and chance for fulfillment.

We could affect the lives of so many people, both spiritually and practically, if we could learn to live the lifestyle of a mentor. We could recapture so much of our nation and culture if we would, as Christians, accept our responsibility as mentors to this present generation. One generation that is effectively mentored would know how to repeat the process in the generations to come.

Chapter 17

The Principle of Twelve and Multiplication

During a regional cell-church seminar, a pastor asked the question, "As a small church, how do you suggest we get started into the cell-church model?"

I have had to answer this question often and I know now what to say. " Just do what Jesus did," I answered, "Seek out twelve people that you want to be with to develop their spiritual lives, and begin a long-term discipleship relationship with them."

The answer I gave seems like an over simplification of the cell-church structure, but it is the model that Jesus used to reach the world. The Principle of Twelve is the most effective structure for the cell-church. It is not about how many meetings you have to go to, or how fast you can multiply; it is about you and the people you are discipling and bringing into spiritual maturity.

What Is the Principle of Twelve?

The Principle of Twelve is *the art of developing twelve new dynamic spiritual relationships.* The Principle of Twelve is the law of relationships that brings every believer into a mentor/protégé relationship with others in the cell group. The two goals of this relationship are **spiritual intimacy** and **reproduction**, the biblical terminology being, *"Be fruitful and multiply"* (Genesis 1:28).

Spiritual Intimacy
Every believer has the responsibility before God to bear fruit and multiply. True multiplication, in the biblical sense, is not how many people you can get to come to a meeting, but rather, how many individual lives you can influence for Christ. Before there can be spiritual reproduction, there has to be spiritual intimacy. The great revival that we read about in the book of Acts is a story of people going from house to house sharing with family members and neighbors the great things that God was doing in that day. I don't believe for a minute that they were inviting loved ones to a

highly planned evangelistic church production put on by the "arts department."

The converts in the newly born Church of Jesus Christ went directly to the people with whom they had life-long relationships. They were excited about the new spiritual life they had found and wanted to share that life with their loved ones. This began a dynamic spiritual relationship with people they were already close to on the human level. The results were that the church exploded in the number of disciples that were added. They didn't have great church buildings; they met in the marketplace and in the Jewish temples and synagogues, and house to house. Church growth was not restricted by the lack of parking, number of seats in the auditorium, or poor promotional ads in the newspaper. It was, however, totally dependent upon the number of relationships that the new converts had, and the number of new relationships they were willing to develop.

Spiritual intimacy is determined by the commitment that we make to nurture and support each other in the things of Christ. But Jesus spent time, not only instructing His disciples, but also dining with them, ministering alongside them, and praying often with them. Likewise, we must be willing to spend time with the people that we want in our "Twelve," modeling all aspects of life and showing them true friendship. By this process, we reveal ourselves to them.

"Henceforth I call you not servants; for the servant knoweth not what his lord doeth: but I have called you friends; for all things that I have heard of my Father I have made known unto you" (John 15:15). This remarkable degree of intimacy is also evident in the relationship that the Apostle Paul had with Timothy. Notice the fatherly greeting Paul uses. *"To Timothy, my dearly beloved son: Grace, mercy, and peace, from God the Father and Christ Jesus our Lord. I thank God, whom I serve from my forefathers with pure conscience, that without ceasing I have remembrance of thee in my prayers night and day; Greatly desiring to see thee, being mindful of thy tears, that I may be filled with joy"* (II Timothy 1:2-4).

In fact, as we read through the letters of Paul to Timothy, we can see the progression of their mentoring relationship.

I Timothy 1:2-3 *"Unto Timothy, my own son in the faith: Grace, mercy, and peace, from God our Father and Jesus Christ our Lord. As I besought* *thee to abide still at Ephesus, when I went into Macedonia, that thou mightest charge some that they teach no other doctrine."* At this point in the relationship it was primarily instructive.

I Timothy 1:18-19 *"This charge I commit unto thee, son Timothy, according to the prophecies which went before on thee, that thou by them mightest war a good warfare; Holding faith, and a good conscience; which some having put away concerning faith have made shipwreck."* We notice Paul begins to encourage Timothy, making a distinction between him and others whose faith had shipwrecked.

I Timothy 6:20-21 *"O Timothy, keep that which is committed to thy trust, avoiding profane and vain babblings, and oppositions of science falsely so called: Which some professing have erred concerning the faith. Grace be with thee. Amen."* Here we see that Paul had entrusted certain things to Timothy and is depending on him to avoid the heresies that beset others who were once in the faith.

By the time we get to II Timothy 1:2-4, the fatherly greeting quoted earlier, Paul has developed a great love for Timothy, not only for his ministry gift and calling, but for his physical presence. This is the spirit of the Principle of Twelve. But it all culminates with this reproductive revelation:

II Timothy 2:1-2 *"Thou therefore, my son, be strong in the grace that is in Christ Jesus. And the things that thou hast heard of me among many witnesses, the same commit thou to faithful men, who shall be able to teach others also."* We see that this intimate relationship is reproducible in level after level of the human relationships of the people we know. This makes multiplication and church growth unlimited.

Reproduction
Reproduction is the function of every believer to transfer all that God has done in his life to another person. This transference of values, character, priorities, and spiritual fruit takes place in the mentoring process.

Jesus **reproduced** His life and ministry in all of His disciples and then delegated the entire work of the Kingdom to them, including His powerful and miraculous works. *"Verily, verily, I say unto you, He that believeth on me, the works that I do shall he do also; and greater [works] than these shall he do; because I go unto my Father"* (John 14:12).

In the "Great Commission" of Matthew 28:18-20, Jesus outlines the reproductive process:

And Jesus came and spake unto them, saying, *"(18) All power is given unto me in heaven and in earth. (19) Go ye therefore, and teach all nations, baptizing them in the name of the Father, and of the Son, and of the Holy Ghost: (20) Teaching them to observe all things whatsoever I have commanded you: and, lo, I am with you alway, [even] unto the end of the world. Amen."*

The word *teach* in verse 19 is the Greek work *matheteuo*, which literally means "to disciple." Discipleship is the teaching aspect of mentoring and is a necessary part of reproducing Christ in others. Preaching the Gospel and teaching all nations is therefore the reproductive function of every believer.

The Biblical Examples of *Twelve*

Genesis 35:22-26 speaks of the twelve sons of Jacob, which were the twelve tribes of Israel. Also, Genesis 49:28 says, *"All these [are] the twelve tribes of Israel: and this [is it] that their father spake unto them, and blessed them; every one according to his blessing he blessed them."* The number twelve here speaks of the posterity of God's people. This is how He **multiplied** His people.

In Genesis 17:20, God blesses Ishmael with twelve princes. *"And as for Ishmael, I have heard thee: Behold, I have blessed him, and will **make him fruitful**, and will **multiply him exceedingly; twelve princes** shall he beget, and I will make him a great nation."* Again, twelve is God's number for "fruitfulness and multiplication"!

In Luke 9:17, twelve was the number of the abundance left over after the feeding of the 5,000; and in Revelation it was the number of the "manner of fruits" on the Tree of Life for the "healing of the nations."

As we study the number twelve in Scripture, we also begin to understand that God used it as the number of perfect government. At the altar that Moses built in Exodus 24:4, there were *"twelve pillars, according to the twelve tribes of Israel"* where Moses reminded the people of God's covenant with Israel. A very similar scene is repeated in Revelation 21:14:

"And the wall of the city had twelve foundations, and in them the names of the twelve apostles of the Lamb." God governed His people through the twelve tribes of Israel and will govern the New Jerusalem with the twelve apostles.

In the New Testament we find that twelve represents the number of discipleship. Jesus chose twelve to work with Him in the carrying out of His ministry on earth and left that ministry in their charge to carry on after He departed. In Matthew 10:1 we read, *"And when he had called unto [him] his twelve disciples, he gave them power [against] unclean spirits, to cast them out, and to heal all manner of sickness and all manner of disease."* Twelve is the number of discipleship. In Acts 19:5-7 the Apostle Paul transfers the gift of the Holy Spirit to twelve men to carry on the ministry in the power of God's Spirit.

As we consider the significance of the number twelve, we see that Scripture applies it to God's government, fruitfulness and multiplication, the posterity of His people, and discipleship. The question that we need to answer is "How does this apply to the cell church?"

The Bogotá Model

In Bogotá, Colombia, Pastor César Castellanos has used the principle of twelve to build a fast growing cell church with over 12,500 groups. His youth pastor, César Fajardo, introduced this principle to the youth ministry in 1991. For two years before this principle was employed, there was little or no cell growth. Fajardo started with his youth group and has since built 6,000 youth cell groups that continue to flourish in the midst of a great revival that is, at this writing, ongoing. The church adopted the principle of twelve to contain the harvest and could soon be the world's largest church.[1]

The Principle of Twelve As it Relates to the Cell Church

The principle of twelve in the New Testament is defined by the lifestyle of Jesus and His disciples. It reaches far beyond just having a leadership structure; **it is a relationship of twelve men with their mentor.** It is a

---

[1] Information provided through César Castellanos, *Liderazgo de Exito a Través de los 12,* Editorial Vilit & Cia. Ltdal., Santa Fe de Bogotá, D.C., Colombia, Sudamérica, 1999.

relationship where all involved shared in intimacy, and each one was totally accountable to the other for his actions and words. They had their shortcomings: Peter when he boasted, James and John when they wanted to take revenge, Philip telling Jesus they needed to see the Father instead. But the presence of their mentor, Jesus, warning them about their mistakes and providing correction, is the key element. The disciples felt at ease to be themselves in His presence. Jesus raised them up to be great leaders in an environment of trust and safety. They were challenged to great things that were beyond human ability, but having been with Jesus, they knew that they could do these things. It is in this light that we approach the Principle of Twelve.

Jesus' Example — *"And he ordained twelve, that they should be with him, and that he might send them forth to preach, and to have power to heal sicknesses, and to cast out devils"* (Mark 3:14).

The first revelation in this passage is that Jesus "ordained" twelve. This indicates to us that He appointed twelve for His own purposes. These men were handpicked. Though not perfect, each one had a purpose to fulfill in Jesus' ministry, even Judas! The fact that He chose twelve is evidence enough for me that the number of discipleship cannot be any other than twelve. Someone asked me once, "Can it be seven?" It can start with one, two or three, but our goal should be twelve in our lifetime.

Secondly, look at the simple purpose revealed here: *"...that they should be with him..."* This means that they should be in His presence. The principle of twelve is a principle of building friendships with the people that you want to be with. It has everything to do with banding together and growing together. It is a partnership of people who want to be together to do whatever God is requiring them to do.

Next, it is a relationship of people who are being "sent forth" together to preach, heal the sick, and cast out devils. It is an active participation in the deliverance and salvation of all who come in contact with this group of twelve. The group is defined by those they are with and what they are doing. In the case of the apostles, it was not just a meeting for the sake of fellowship or just to meet the needs of those in the group, but to bring Christ to the people of the cities and towns to which they would travel.

Is it a multilevel principle of productivity? Let me put it this way. It is not a CEO structure of productivity only! It is a principle of "relationship discipleship" made up of people who love each other and are committed to each other regardless of their abilities. Productivity comes from the love that is expressed within the group. This is a structure that first meets the needs of those within the group then empowers them to reach out to regions beyond the group. Let's look specifically at the threefold purpose of the relationships.

• Meet the need of the members of the group.

• Empower the people to do greater works.

• Send them out to reach others.

Throughout the New Testament, Jesus broke the legalistic structure of the Pharisees and Sadducees. They demanded the letter of the law, but when He healed on the Sabbath time and again, He taught them the law of compassion. *"And the ruler of the synagogue answered with indignation, because that Jesus had healed on the sabbath day, and said unto the people, There are six days in which men ought to work: in them therefore come and be healed, and not on the sabbath day"* (Luke 13:14).

We cannot limit the meaning of the principle of twelve to only a fast church-growth method. It is, however, an agreement between everyone in each group to take the city by means of serving each other and the community they live in. How? By demonstrating the love of Christ. An attitude of "My twelve and I are going to change this city" is the passion that should develop within the group.

The circle of Twelve — Is it a meeting? Of course, the principle of twelve requires that the members meet together as a "circle" group on a weekly basis, but it is not confined to a meeting. The meeting is a time where spiritual gifts are deployed, vision and purpose defined or reiterated, and where the heart of the senior pastor is passed down through the mentoring network. But the discipleship process of the principle of twelve continues on a daily basis between the members and the mentors. Whatever the needs of the group are, they are addressed day to day and house to house by each member of the group. The circle of twelve meets to be edified, then goes out to build up the church.

Two meetings take less time than one — This seems to be a contradiction, so let me explain.

Jesus always prepared His disciples before He sent them out to minister. In the same way a mentor must prepare his leaders before they lead their weekly groups. This requires two meetings per week. Since time is the greatest commodity of the 21st Century, how will it be possible to get that kind of participation?

First, realize that for someone to prepare the lesson and get insights to share in his/her own meeting requires several hours of time. However, when they attend their mentor's meeting, they hear the lesson being presented, gain useful insights, and can ask questions to clear up any issues. After a standard ninety-minute meeting, they are ready to go lead their own group.

The second meeting is the one that the leader facilitates with his/her group. He has gained the necessary information from his/her mentor and is now ready to pass that information on to the group. It is much less time consuming to gather the group members together than to track down each one separately to go over the lesson with them. Try to contact twelve people next week to arrange a meeting or even a telephone conversation with them. It is nearly impossible. By having a meeting with them that lasts ninety minutes, you can share the lesson, pray for and minister to each one, then set up times that you can get together with the ones who need personal attention.

Jesus and His Twelve — After Jesus chose His disciples (Mark 3:14, Matthew 4:18-22), He began a relationship with them that would change the world of His day and the entire course of history. The points below reveal to us His master plan to usher in the Kingdom of God on earth.

• **By being baptized, He expressed submission to follow righteousness** — *"Then cometh Jesus from Galilee to Jordan unto John, to be baptized of him. But John forbade him, saying, 'I have need to be baptized of thee, and comest thou to me?' And Jesus answering said unto him, 'Suffer [it to be so] now: for thus it becometh us to fulfil all righteousness.' Then he suffered him"* (Matthew 3:13-15).

• **He called them to make them leaders** — *"And He said to them, 'Follow* *me and I will make you fishers of men'"* (Matthew 4:19). Jesus saw potential for the Kingdom of God in every soul that He met. His disciples would be His inner circle. He chose them by offering them purpose.

- **He chose diverse men with different backgrounds** — The disciples were fishermen, tax collectors, and common men. He called the rich and poor, common and uncommon, educated and uneducated into His twelve.

- **He made His selection after intense prayer** — *"And it came to pass in those days, that He went out into a mountain to pray, and continued all night in prayer to God. And when it was day, He called [unto him] his disciples: and of them he chose twelve, whom also He named apostles"* (Luke 6:12-13).

Jesus' Strategy for Training and Developing His Twelve Disciples

- **He taught them privately** — *"After Jesus had finished instructing His twelve disciples, He went on from there to teach and preach in the towns of Galilee"* (Matthew 11:1, NIV).

- **He taught them on a privileged level** — *"When He was alone, the Twelve and the others around Him asked Him about the parables. He told them, 'The secret of the kingdom of God has been given to you. But to those on the outside everything is said in parables...'"* (Mark 4:10-11, NIV). Notice that after ministering to the multitudes, Jesus always sent them away.

- **He taught them by demonstration** — *"After this, Jesus traveled about from one town and village to another, proclaiming the good news of the kingdom of God. The Twelve were with Him"* (Luke 8:1).

- **He shared His intimate life with them** — *"We are going up to Jerusalem, and the Son of Man will be betrayed to the chief priests and the teachers of the law. They will condemn him to death"* (Matthew 20:18, NIV).

- **He lived with them** — *"When evening came, Jesus was reclining at the* *table with the Twelve"* (Matthew 26:20, NIV).

- **He was open with them** — *"And while they were eating, He said, 'I tell you the truth, one of you will betray me'"* (Matthew 26:21, NIV).

- **He delegated the responsibility of leadership to them** — *"And He ordained twelve, that they should be with Him, and that He might send them forth to preach, and to have power to heal sicknesses, and to cast out devils"* (Mark 3:14-15). He delegated authority to them and released them. He gave them specific instructions. *"Take nothing for the journey—no staff, no bag, no bread, no money, no extra tunic. Whatever house you enter, stay there until you leave that town"* (Luke 9:3-4, NIV).

- **He demanded extreme levels of personal sacrifice** — The disciples were asked to forsake their families, careers, and property. *"Peter said to him, 'We have left all we had to follow you'"* (Luke 18:28, NIV).

- **He asked for a lifelong allegiance** — *"For whosoever will save his life shall lose it; but whosoever shall lose his life for my sake and the gospel's, the same shall save it"* (Mark 8:35).

He allowed for levels of relationships:

- **The multitude and disciples** — *"He went down with them and stood on a level place. A large crowd of his disciples was there and a great number of people from all over Judea, from Jerusalem, and from the coast of Tyre and Sidon"* (Luke 6:17, NIV).

- **The seventy** — *"After this the Lord appointed seventy others and sent them two by two ahead of him to every town and place where he was about to go"* (Luke 10:1, NIV).

- **The Twelve** — *"And it came to pass, when Jesus had made an end of commanding His twelve disciples, He departed thence to teach and to preach in their cities"* (Matthew 11:1).

- **The inner circle** — Peter, James and John *"And after six days Jesus taketh Peter, James, and John his brother, and bringeth them up into an high mountain apart…"* (Matthew 17:1).

• **He paired them together in ministry partnerships** — *"Calling the Twelve to him, he sent them out two by two..."* (Mark 6:7).

He served them — *"Ye call me Master and Lord: and ye say well; for [so] I am. If I then, [your] Lord and Master, have washed your feet; ye also ought to wash one another's feet. For I have given you an example, that ye should do as I have done to you"* (John 13:13-15).

He forgave them — *"And the Lord said, 'Simon, Simon, behold, Satan hath desired [to have] you, that he may sift [you] as wheat: But I have prayed for thee, that thy faith fail not: and when thou art converted, strengthen thy brethren"* (Luke 22:31-32). In every discipleship relationship there will be opportunity to correct, forgive, encourage, and move on in leadership.

By studying Jesus' relationship with the Twelve, we discover the full scope of their development. What a challenge it is to us to replicate this intense pattern of discipleship. But think what it would mean to the young Christians in our midst if we would commit to each one in the way Christ did for His disciples.

The Multiplication Principle of Twelve

Multiplication is essential because each group is only one generation from extinction. Think about that for a moment. It's a vital principle to understand.

Why Not the 5x5, Jethro Model?

When we first started cell groups at Bethany, we used the 5x5 model that is sometimes called the Jethro model. It was set up to provide one leader and one intern with each group. The group would grow to 12 – 15 members then multiply with the intern taking half of the group with him/her.

Two major problems with this system began to emerge. First of all, nobody wanted to separate from the relationships that they had in the group; and secondly, only one person was really focused on as a leader.

With the Principle of Twelve (G-12 model), relationships stay intact and everyone is viewed as a potential leader. This makes multiplication potential twelve times more possible.

With groups dividing constantly, new leadership is less mature with every multiplication in the 5x5 model. However, in the G-12 model, leadership has time to mature and grow in skill as he/she is constantly being mentored.

Three Aspects of the Principle of Twelve

These need to be clearly defined and understood before we review the multiplication process.

- *Principle of Twelve*—As previously discussed, it is the principle of mentoring.

- *Circle of Twelve*—Also mentioned, it is the actual cell meeting.

- *Permanent Twelve*—To be discussed here, it is the leaders that each cell leader develops and assumes a mentoring role with for a "permanent" duration.

The Goal of Multiplication

- Reproduce the life and vision of the local church through cell groups

- Reproduce leaders

- Multiply without destroying relationships.

Five Groups from Which to Draw Your Twelve

The question is asked, "Where do I get my twelve from?" The answer is the same as those you should mentor. Remember these five areas?

- Draw from people that you already have a close relationship with and that you want to be with.

- Draw from people that you would like to have a relationship with because you see potential in them.

- Find people whose needs you want to meet.

- You may include people that approach you and ask to be in your twelve. (This happens more often than you think.)

- Include the friends of members in your group that the member believes would benefit from being a part of your group.

When every person in your church embraces the Principle of Twelve, no matter how long it takes, it will open your church to the dynamic of Jesus' ministry style and His plan for reaching the world. Do you realize that if each person would add two new spiritual relationships to their lives in the next twelve months, we would see an explosion in the membership of the local church?

You begin by serving those that you already have a relationship with, by loving them with the love of Christ and making yourself available to them to meet their needs. Love multiplies every attempt we make at reaching people. Prayerfully consider whom God would connect your life with in a strong spiritual bond. Then, begin dynamic, growing, and intentional relationships. These will produce great rewards for a lifetime and also throughout eternity.

Chapter 18

The Challenge and the Charge

The Challenge

What's Seems to Be the Problem?

That's just it, there is a fundamental and limiting problem experienced by American churches today, and we must solve it: *Why can't our churches grow? Why is it that we stay the same while the world around us changes and grows?* We read every day about new technologies that explode on the world scene and gain instant notoriety, but our local churches have been around for decades and are all but ignored. The challenge is to fix the problem of stagnation and boredom throughout the church. A report by the *McAlvany Intelligence Advisor*, which came to me via an e-mail attachment, reveals that **four thousand churches close each year in the U.S. due to the <u>lack of community</u>. Three thousand people leave the church every day, committed not to return because of the <u>lack of purpose</u>**. Eighty-five percent of all churches in the U.S. have reached a plateau or are decreasing in attendance. Friends, we *must* change the way we "do" church!

Someone once defined "insanity" as, "Doing the same thing over and over again and expecting different results!" That definition begs the following question: Is what you are doing working? If it isn't, doing it harder, longer, with more energy and with more people will not bring success. The answer is to do something different, something that *works*. Find another method that holds the promise of growth and expansion for your church and ministry. Be willing to risk some of what you are holding onto in order to gain the growth that is currently eluding your grasp. Exchange complacency for urgency, status quo for strategy, and paralysis for productivity. Expose the problem that has held up the church and make that problem the reason for change.

People won't move if they don't sense that there is a problem. You can't let your congregation have the mentality that all is well when it isn't. You can't keep making excuses for why the church doesn't grow. Realize that the programs in the church have failed to add new souls, failed to make disciples, and failed to raise up new motivated leaders. Your church may be existing on "old cheese." Find the new cheese and go get it![1]

The Chance for Growth Requires the Risk of Change

Improvement, learning, growth are all results of change. With each there is an uncertainty, a risk. But we must face the uncertainties with faith and flexibility. Flexibility is the prerequisite of opportunity. Opportunity can not be accessed by rigid or stiff people. How many times are promotions lost by people unwilling to accept the changes their corporation is making. The same is true of the Church. If we are not willing to risk the status quo, we will never know what the rewards of growth can be.

The cell-church structure requires a major change in how we think of church. It may require the cessation of many familiar programs that have been the pillars of your church. But the challenge to grow and reach your city or town for Christ may be beckoning you to take a look at the possibilities the cell church has to offer.

The Need for Inventors

Around the world, major corporations employ huge Research and Development (R&D) departments. Think of the billions of dollars and millions of man-hours spent on the develop of AIDS vaccinations and other new drugs, on computer software, on the engineering of aerospace vehicles, and on operating systems for almost every emerging industry and business. Microsoft scoured Planet Earth to find the most qualified computer scientists and inventors in its field for the purpose of research and development of new systems.

So, where are the inventors in the church? Society is reengineering and reinventing itself every three years. A church that reinvents itself every thirty years has lost touch with its society and will never catch up without invention. The challenge is before us. We need Christian leaders who are always on a quest, not only to improve present programs, but to create and/or invent new ways of reaching a constantly changing society.

---

[1] The term comes from the book by Dr. Spencer Johnson, *Who Moved My Cheese?*, G. P. Putnam's Sons, New York, New York, 1998.

The Charge

In October of 1854, during the Crimean War, a joint force of over 60,000 troops from Britain, France, and Turkey faced off with Russian troops at Balaklava in the Ukraine. After removing the Turks from the Causeway Heights where British guns were left behind, the Russians troops occupied the hills around what would become known as the "Valley of Death."

What happened next has gone down as one of the greatest, noblest, and perhaps most misguided military actions in British history. A misstated or perhaps misunderstood order ended up sending the British Light Brigade on a military charge that has gone down in history for its gallantry. The Light Brigade was an elite force of the British Calvary that numbered about 600 men. It is debatable, since the Light Brigade acted upon the orders and attacked towards the wrong direction, if the action was to be rewarded or condemned, but the spirit and courage of the Light Brigade is to be commended and even emulated. Each member of the Light Brigade was eventually honored and awarded the "Balaklava Clasp" for their actions. This action changed the course of the battle and eventually led to victory for the British, French, and Turkish troops.

Not necessarily for the course of events in the historical accounts of the charge of the Light Brigade, but for its tremendous motivation for victory, I would like to close with the stirring poem written by Alfred, Lord Tennyson, "The Charge of the Light Brigade." [2] This poem represents a risk taken by a brigade *in carrying out a commandment.*

---

[2] Taken from *Poetry for Pleasure, The Hallmark Book of Poetry,* Doubleday & Company, Inc. New York, 1960.

The Charge of the Light Brigade

Alfred, Lord Tennyson

Half a league, half a league,
Half a league onward,
All in the valley of Death
    Rode the six hundred.
"Forward, the Light Brigade!
Charge for the guns!" he said:
Into the valley of Death
    Rode the six hundred.

"Forward, the Light Brigade!"
Was there a man dismayed?
Not though the soldier knew
    Some one had blundered:
Theirs not to make reply,
Theirs not to reason why,
Theirs but to do and die:
Into the valley of Death
    Rode the six hundred.

Cannon to right of them,
Cannon to left of them,
Cannon in front of them
    Volleyed and thundered;
Stormed at with shot and shell,
Boldly they rode and well,
Into the jaws of Death,
Into the mouth of Hell
    Rode the six hundred.

Flashed all their sabres bare,
Flashed as they turned in air

Sabring the gunners there,
Charging an army, while
    All the world wondered:
Plunged in the battery-smoke
Right through the line they broke;
Cossack and Russian
Reeled from the sabre-stroke
    Shattered and sundered.
Then they rode back, but not,
    Not the six hundred.

Cannon to right of them,
Cannon to left of them,
Cannon behind them
    Volleyed and thundered;
Stormed at with shot and shell,
While horse and hero fell,
They that had fought so well
Came through the jaws of Death,
Back from the mouth of Hell,
All that was left of them,
    Left of six hundred.

When can their glory fade?
O the wild charge they made!
    All the world wondered.
Honour the charge they made!
Honour the Light Brigade,
    Noble six hundred!

"Go ye therefore"... Matthew 28:19
Jesus Christ

Contact Info:

Internet:
www.billyhornsby.com
www.missiontips.com
www.relatedchurches.com

E-mail:
billy@missiontips.com
billy@relatedchurches.com

Address:
Billy Hornsby Ministries, Inc.
P.O. Box 78003
Baton Rouge, LA 70837-8003

Phone/Fax (225) 261-0394

BIBLIOGRAPHY

Beckham, William A., *The Second Reformation: Reshaping the Church for the 21st Century,* TOUCH Publications, Houston, Texas, 1995.

Biehl, Bobb, *Mentoring: Confidence in Finding a Mentor and Becoming One*, Broadman and Holman Publishers, Nashville, Tennessee, 1996.

_____, *Stop Setting Goals If You Would Rather Solve Problems,* Ballantine Books, 1995.

Castellanos D., César, *Liderazgo de Exito a Través de los 12*, Editorial Vilit & Cia. Ltda., Santa Fe de Bogotá, D.C., Colombia, Sudamérica, 1999.

Comiskey, Joel, *Home Cell Group Explosion: How Your Small Group Can Grow and Multiply,* Touch Publications, Houston, Texas, 1998.

Donahue, Bill, *Leading Life-Changing Small Groups,* Zondervan Publishing House, Grand Rapids, Michigan, 1996.

Elmore, Tim, *The Greatest Mentors in the Bible: 32 Relationships Used to Change the World*, Kingdom Publishing House, Denver, Colorado, 1996.

Gerber, Michael, *The E Myth Revisited: Why Most Small Businesses Don't Work and What to Do About It*, HarperCollins Publishers, Inc., New York, New York, 1995.

Good Stuff, Progressive Business Publications, Malvern, Pennsylvania, February 2000.

Green, Michael, *Evangelism in the Early Church*, Eagle, Guildford, Surrey, U.K., 1970.

Hattingh, Suzette, *Intercession as a Lifestyle Video Series*, Distributed by: Marilyn Neubauer, P. O. Box 302, Vista, California 92085.

Hurston, Karen, *Growing the World's Largest Church*, Gospel Publishing House, Springfield, Missouri, 1994.

Johnson, Spencer, *Who Moved My Cheese?*, G. P. Putnam's Sons, New York, New York, 1998.

Kotter, John P., *Leading Change*, Harvard Business School Press, Boston, Massachusetts, 1996.

Krieder, Larry, *House to House: Spiritual Insights for the 21st Century Church*, House to House Publications, Ephrata, Pennsylvania, 1995.

Maxwell, John, "Leadership is Influence", Injoy Leadership Seminar, Alexandria, Louisiana, October 27 and 28, 1997.

McAlvany, Donald S., *McAlvany Intelligence Advisor*, www.mcalvany.com.

Neighbour, Ralph W., Jr., *Where Do We Go From Here? A Guidebook for Cell Group Churches*, Touch Publications, Inc., Houston, Texas, 1990.

_____ , *The Shepherd's Guidebook*, Touch Publications, Inc., Houston, Texas, 1988.

Pritchett, Price, *Firing Up Commitment During Organizational Change*, Pritchett and Associates, Dallas, Texas, 1994.

Schuller, Robert, *Your Church Has a Fantastic Future*, Regal Books, Ventura, California, 1986.

Schwarz, Christian A., *Natural Church Development*, M.C.E. HOREB, Viladecavalls (Barcelona), Spain, 1996.

Wagner, C. Peter, *Your Spiritual Gifts Can Help Your Church Grow*, Regal Books, Ventura, California, 1994.

Ziglar, Zig, *Top Performance*, Berkley Books, New York, New York, 1986.

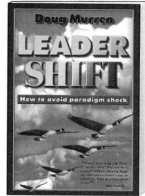